As Leaders Learn

D0071636

A joint publication of the Danforth Foundation,
the College of Education at the University of Maine,
and Corwin Press, Inc.

As Leaders Learn

Personal Stories of Growth in School Leadership

Editors:
Gordon A. Donaldson Jr.
George F. Marnik

CORWIN PRESS, INC.
A Sage Publications Company
Thousand Oaks, California

For information address:

Corwin Press, Inc.
2455 Teller Road
Thousand Oaks, California 91320

SAGE Publications Ltd.
6 Bonhill Street
London EC2A 4PU
United Kingdom

SAGE Publications India Pvt. Ltd.
M-32 Market
Greater Kailash I
New Delhi 110 048 India

Printed in the United States of America

Library of Congress Cataloging-in-Publication Data

As leaders learn: personal stories of growth in school leadership/
editors, Gordon A. Donaldson, Jr., George F. Marnik.
   p. cm.
Includes bibliographical references.
ISBN 0-8039-6301-7 (cloth).—ISBN 0-8039-6302-5 (pbk.)
1. Educational leadership—Maine. I. Donaldson, Gordon A., Jr.
II. Marnik, George F.
LB2805.A67 1995
   371.2—dc20   95-7972

This book is printed on acid-free paper.

95 96 97 98 99 10 9 8 7 6 5 4 3 2 1

Corwin Press Production Editor: S. Marlene Head

CONTENTS

FOREWORD
The Voices of Practicing School Leaders

You are about to read a remarkable collection of stories. They are remarkable in their clarity, drama, and passion. They are remarkable in their insight. Most of all, they are remarkable because these are the voices of practicing school leaders—both teachers and principals—revealing the often murky, mysterious, and very important world of public school leadership.

The knowledge base of school reform is thought to reside in large-scale social science research studies, with the efforts of academics such as John Goodlad, Ted Sizer, James Comer, and Mortimer Adler. And indeed, these and others outside the schools who would transform the nature and quality of public education have much to offer. But an equally powerful and important knowledge base for school improvement can be found among the adults who live and work under the schoolhouse roofs. The teachers, administrators, guidance counselors, and many parents who work with youngsters—and with one another—necessarily accumulate tremendous insights and information about how schools function. They know volumes about curriculum development, teaching, organizing youngsters, involving parents, staff development, and school leadership—the stuff of school reform.

Unfortunately, in most school cultures, taboos do not often permit school practitioners to reveal their abundant craft knowledge to one another, let alone to the outside world. A treasure trove of wisdom lies within frontline practitioners, hermetically sealed and largely unavailable to the crucial work of school improvement. What a tragic loss—to the profession, to the professionals, and to the process of personal, professional, and institutional renewal.

If the craft knowledge of the schoolhouse residents is seldom made audible, it is even less common for it to be revealed in writing. Writing about school practice is, as we say, "at risk." There is no discretionary time for those who work in schools to reflect and to write. One person's craft knowledge can risk offending colleagues who would invariably tell the story differently. And it brings under scrutiny not only the content but the quality of the writing of those entrusted to educate and to teach writing to young people. In short, for school practitioners to write about the treasures they hold about the school world makes them very vulnerable indeed.

I first became acquainted with the work of this volume's practitioner-authors when invited to read versions of the manuscripts you are about to read prior to meeting with the group one splendid summer day in Round Pond, Maine. My assignment was to offer helpful feedback. This was an experience far too rare in our profession: a conversation about writing about school practice among practitioners.

I was moved by the courage of these educators and by what they had to say. Their words are at times artistic, at times polished; sometimes they are uneven and halting. At all times, however, they are honest. Their message does not replace the academic knowledge base about school improvement. Rather, I find the craft knowledge of these and other practitioners forcefully challenges, extends, questions, and complements the research. Together, the two literatures inform one another and together they form a rich resource to school practitioners.

I was honored to be invited into the world of these practitioner-writers through their description and analysis of practice. I suspect you, too, will feel honored to be permitted in. There is much for all of us to learn here.

ROLAND BARTH
Alna, Maine

WELCOME

We offer the stories in this small volume to fellow seekers after an elusive dream—that schools can and must function more productively and humanely for children and adults. We are nine Maine educators who have banded together to help each other meet the challenges of leading schools toward this dream. Together we have explored the puzzles inherent in this process and helped each other understand how we can become more effective leaders.

We are teacher leaders, teaching principals, and principals. We met in January 1992 in a federally supported leadership development program called the Maine Academy for School Leaders (MASL) that is described in a partner book, *Becoming Better Leaders: The Challenge of Improving Student Learning* (Corwin, 1995). In the years since that time, we and other Maine school leaders have worked to improve our understanding and practice of leadership. With support from the Danforth Foundation, the schools and districts of the participants, and the University of Maine, in December of 1993 we established a Writers' Collaborative. The personal stories in this volume are the first products of the monthly gatherings of the Collaborative.

Our writing has had one goal: to make sense of some of the toughest leadership challenges we face so we can see more clearly how we should lead. "Our Journey: Notes From the Writers' Collaborative Log" (p. 81) describes our activities and how we assisted one another to address these challenges. "Writing for Professional Growth: A Double-Edged Sword" (p. 93) examines some pitfalls we encountered in the writing process itself. Our writings have benefited from long conversations, support, trust, empathy, and humor. We hope that you, whether you face such challenges yourself or work in leadership development programs, will find them helpful.

Our stories are as varied as our group and our schools. Some follow efforts to forge teams of faculty groups that are divided over educational philosophy and by personal histories. Others trace attempts to respond more constructively to angry or demanding parents and colleagues. Still others mark, through personal reflection on our professional careers, the twists and turns of our evolving identities as leaders.

And our stories strike common chords. We all struggle with raising the stakes in schools where both educators and citizens find the status quo more appetizing than change. We all face interpersonal quandaries as others resist our efforts: To collaborate or compel? To confront or to connive? To trust or to distrust our colleagues' motives? And we all wonder whether the investment of time, care, and energy inherent in leading (and the debt incurred to our personal time and families) are worth it.

As you read, you will encounter terminology from the Leadership Academy. We have included a glossary of MASL terms at the end of the book (see p. 99).

We wish to thank Peter Wilson at the Danforth Foundation and Dean Robert Cobb of the College of Education at the University of Maine for their support of this work. We are also indebted to each of the districts in which these school leaders work. Publically sharing the intimate challenges of school leadership is a risk to many of us— but one that demonstrates a commitment to personal and professional growth. Without Amy Cates's agile fingers and creative flair, the manuscript would never have come together as it has. And finally, we thank Cary Donaldson whose sketch of the "blooming schoolhouse" is the Maine Network for School Leaders logo.

For those who work with school leaders through university and other professional development opportunities, we hope the concept of exploring leadership issues through writing intrigues you with the possibilities of such sharing and collegial learning. For those who work in schools and confront the challenges of leadership every day, we hope our stories will help you understand your leadership better in your school. Perhaps, too, they will stimulate you to improve your leadership as we have tried to improve ours.

GORDON A. DONALDSON, JR.
GEORGE F. MARNIK
Editors
Orono, Maine

ABOUT THE AUTHORS

Donald Buckingham is a Teaching Principal at Sedgwick Elementary School. In 1994 he was named Maine's National Distinguished Principal and returned to the "Pretty" River to paddle from its source to Hudson Bay.

Ann Constantine Cheney is Chapter I Coordinator in York, Maine.

Martha G. Corkery, currently a 6th-grade teacher, taught 16 years in secondary schools and earned a Master's Degree in literacy education and principal's credential. She has worked as a consultant in literacy, group process, teacher leadership, and organizational change.

Gordon A. Donaldson, Jr. was the Director of MASL and is a coeditor of this book. He is a Professor at the University of Maine.

Sally Mackenzie taught at a Portland, Maine, area high school and is currently an instructor at Bowdoin College in Brunswick, Maine.

George F. Marnik is a Curriculum Staff Development Coordinator and Assistant Principal in Deer Isle, Maine. George was cofacilitator of the Writers' Collaborative and is a coeditor of this book.

Patrick R. Phillips is Principal of Blue Hill Consolidated School in Blue Hill, Maine.

Norma Richard has served for most of the past 17 years as a teacher and then as Teaching Principal at Penobscot Elementary School in Penobscot, Maine. She lives in Penobscot with her devoted sheltie, Phineas, and her amazing cat, Cagney.

Elizabeth Wiley is a teacher of English at Cape Elizabeth High School in Cape Elizabeth, Maine.

THE MAINE NETWORK OF SCHOOL LEADERS
The Network Mission

For a century and a half, most Maine children attended the many small, rural district schoolhouses that dotted the state's landscape. Although they did not always fully educate all Maine children, these schools often melded children, parents, grandparents, and teacher in a community of interest that reinforced neighborhood identities and challenged and celebrated children. Within the lifetimes of current Mainers, schooling has moved to large, compartmentalized facilities serving several towns at once. New leadership is required if these schools are to foster community and challenge and celebrate children as district schoolhouses did.

The Maine Network for School Leaders' logo symbolizes both the breaking away from the structures of schooling and the flowering of the best child-centered teaching from Maine's educational past. The Network seeks to move beyond the artifice of imposed structure and in its place nurture educational processes and practices that will bring the talents and human capacities of our children into bloom.

The Maine Network of School Leaders welcomes all those who have committed themselves to the personal and professional change necessary to move Maine schools forward in this manner. In the place of old habits and ineffective concepts and behaviors of leadership, the Network invites leaders to explore ways to make their own beliefs and behaviors influence both adults' and children's attitudes and practices so that children's learning is enhanced.

As leaders learn, so will those they lead. Network members strive to make themselves blossom so that others will blossom. The Maine Network of School Leaders is a community intentionally fashioning a culture for the spread of sound learning principles and practices for all Maine schools, their adults, and their children.

The MNSL philosophy and developmental process for leadership development are described in *Becoming Better Leaders* by Gordon A. Donaldson, Jr. and George F. Marnik, published in 1995 by Corwin Press. If you are interested in learning more about the Network, please contact Gordon Donaldson (207-581-2450) or George Marnik (207-348-2705).

CONFLICT WITH MRS. Z:
Lessons From an Unlikely Source

*A teaching principal confronts a disruptive parent—and her own
avoidance of conflict—and learns how constructive conflict can be.*

Norma Richard

Why one parent, Mrs. Z, holds the power to push my buttons both
angers and perplexes me. I have avoided her to the full extent of my
avoidance behaviors and have accommodated her when forced to face
her barrage of complaints. This mother has roamed my hallways and
my dreams and I nearly always feel emotionally drained for days prior
to our meetings, and for days after them. If I were awarding a certifi-
cate for the most parent meetings with the principal, then Mrs. Z would
be the obvious winner. Most complaints by a parent? You've guessed
it; Mrs. Z wins hands down. Let's make it a total sweep and also award
her the prize for being the single, most constant source of stress from
a parent that I have experienced as principal over the past 5 years.

Most parents share concerns at one time or another about their
child's classroom, school work, or teacher. Mrs. Z was infamous for
voicing her complaints to me, to the community at large, or to anyone

who would listen, about her children's schooling or, for that matter, any other child's school experiences.

> "Isn't it bizarre that the first graders don't have desks and
>   work at tables?"
> "Why aren't all the children in second grade on the same
>   page in math?"
> "Duty teachers don't help my son with his problems at recess.
>   That is why he misbehaves and doesn't respect teachers."

She was instrumental in forcing one teacher to resign midyear and physically threatened another teacher not once, but twice, stating "I am so mad at you I could punch you." She made excuses for her children's behaviors while complaining that there was little or no discipline at school and that teachers were not consistent in disciplining. Her son was not being challenged and his discipline problems stemmed from his boredom. We were not using the right materials with her daughter.

Teachers were always at fault, and she believed everything that her children told her when they came home from school. Teachers were advised never to confer with her alone, and I took to assisting in classrooms whenever she came to "visit" in order to protect my colleagues' sanity and their reputations. Our conferences after her classroom "visits" were especially stressful as her comments and observations were so very negative, in contrast to my positive and optimistic view of our school and our work with children. My only relief in dealing with her was the support and sympathy I received from my staff. But that didn't even begin to counteract the stress that occurred whenever she was around.

Yet, when I woke at 5:00 a.m. on January 14 , 1993, I knew that the day's scheduled meeting with Mrs. Z would be substantially different from those in the past. I felt rested and at ease. I still felt the need to dress in my best "confident administrator" outfit that morning: tailored navy blue suit, dark hose and heels, and new silk blouse. But I enjoyed a wonderful breakfast of waffles (frozen, but a big improvement over a bagel on the run) and strawberries, taking the time to sit at the table for what could be considered a leisurely breakfast on an early work day. Meditating before I left for school enhanced my peaceful inner tone and my positive feelings.

So, what accounted for this change in my feelings before this parent meeting? Why was January 14 so very different from other meetings over the past 5 years when I longed to fabricate elaborate excuses in order to postpone or cancel this woman's inevitable litany of complaints about my colleagues and me? The answers can be found in what accompanied me on this day to school and to the 10:30 appointment with Mrs. Z. For you see, I felt that I did not start this day or enter this meeting alone. Along with me were the teachings of David Sanderson*, the wisdom of Stephen Covey, and the support of the MASL colleagues who have championed and nurtured my professional growth over the past 2 years.

Conflict Can Be Constructive if I Make It So

David Sanderson's work has been an essential part of this search for personal growth as it has enabled me to develop a more realistic picture of the role of conflict in my life. It has helped me to recognize that conflict can be both essential and healthy for an organization. That recognition actually started at a 2-day MASL session in March 1992. Our last activity on Friday night, before breaking to socialize, was to complete a conflict management style survey designed to identify six different styles for managing conflict: persuading, compelling, avoiding/accommodating, collaborating, negotiating, and supporting. It was getting late, I was tired, and for some reason I was not very excited about this task. A cold beer was on my mind and I could not wait for our group to finish the survey. After scoring the survey, I found myself showing the strongest preference for the avoidance/accommodation strategies for conflict management. Initially I felt that the survey results were somehow inaccurate and my first reactions that night were very strong. "This can't be right. I don't avoid conflict. It's late. I'm tired. I don't really like this survey, and when are we going to break so I can have a beer."

After some reflection, I came to realize that there was a lot more truth to these results than I originally cared to acknowledge. I am

---

*David Sanderson is an organizational consultant living in Lamoine, Maine. His address is: RFD #2, Eagle Point, Ellsworth, ME 04605.

identified as the peacemaker in my family and am known to take all conflicts personally, whether they involve me or not. I very often find myself, personally and professionally, working from what I consider to be a proactive stance in order to avoid conflicts. I rationalize that it is more effective to deal with issues or concerns before they become full-fledged problems. This rationalization comes from my being very uncomfortable with conflicts and my feelings that I am less than successful dealing with them. I am especially quick to avoid conflict when emotions come into play. By operating in the avoidance/accommodation style, I believed that downplaying or eliminating conflict would result in a smoother, safer environment.

I am learning, beginning with my MASL experiences, that conflict is an integral part of our professional lives and an essential component for individual growth. It can provide potential for an organization or group to move in a new direction. I am also more aware that I can and do employ a variety of strategies to deal with conflict more effectively. At times I may resolve differences collaboratively, working with parents to resolve a difficult issue with a student. I may compel or use the authority in my position, as I did when my custodian had a concern that he took to the school committee before he spoke to me. Or, I may bargain, achieving a compromise with my cooks when initiating a salad bar program. And I still may avoid, choosing not to deal with a difficult parent face-to-face when such a meeting has no purpose other than to be confrontational.

David Sanderson's work with MASL, beginning with his workshop on June 24, 1992, and continuing at the Bowdoin Summer Institute a month later, outlined for me the need to support and even value conflict. This was not easy for me to accept as it stands in stark contrast to my preferred style of dealing with conflict. But I am gaining a more comprehensive understanding that conflict is an inherent part of any organization and that it is often healthier for one to deal with it rather than avoid or ignore it. Expanding my repertoire of conflict management skills to include more than my preferred strategy of avoid/accommodate has been a goal for me over the past 2 years. My growing understanding gave me confidence as I approached the January 14 meeting with Mrs. Z. I was ready and, believe it or not, even eager to confront and deal with her conflict-generating behaviors.

Be Responsible for My Behaviors, Not Others'

But I carried another partner with me that day: Stephen Covey. My copy of *The Seven Habits of Highly Effective People* is well worn (Covey, 1990). Covey's work has over the past 2 years provided me with a much welcomed framework for clarifying my personal values and goals. In very many ways this book has been a guide to intrapersonal growth as well as to improved interpersonal relationships. It has been a strong influence in my life as I am experiencing the power of personal change.

Covey (1990) writes, "If I really want to improve my situation, I can work on the one thing over which I have control—myself. I can stop trying to shape my life and work on my own weaknesses . . . the most positive way I can influence my situation is to work on myself, on my being" (p. 90). Upon first reading this, I literally felt a tremendous burden lifted from my shoulders. Covey was reminding me that the only behaviors I had control over were my own.

Such a simple concept, but one with a tremendous amount of truth in it! I do let people, like Mrs. Z, get to me, and I have done it all of my life. I wake up at night thinking about what she might say or do, what bomb will she drop during public comments at our next board meeting. I feel guilty. Have I let my staff down? Have I done enough to protect them from her attacks and accusations? What else could I have done? I think of ways to make things better. I take a strong reactive stance, cover all of my bases, and pour a tremendous amount of energy into trying to control the actions of other people.

During my MASL experiences, and continuing through the past school year, I have worked hard to develop a sense of self-control. I am seeing how changes in my behaviors, actions, and attitudes over the past year have opened leadership doors for colleagues and even sustained important relationships with friends and family through some difficult times. They have helped me deal more effectively with conflict as I gain a better sense of responsibility—or as Covey (1990) writes, "response-ability"—and interact in more proactive and positive ways (p. 71). They have reminded me that I do not have control over the community and that a defeat in the school budget at town meeting is not my fault. They have reminded me that I do not have control over my sisters' behaviors and that I am responsible only for my having a good time at family gatherings. They have reminded me that I do not have control over Mrs. Z's behavior and that I can take responsibility only for my behaviors towards her.

This focus on taking a more proactive role in all aspects of my life has made me feel very powerful indeed. In his book, Covey (1990) shares a quote from Eleanor Roosevelt: "No one can make you feel inferior without your consent" (p. 72). I cannot adequately communicate how this one quote has impacted my life over the past year. In it, I have discovered a tremendous amount of both power and relief. I was thus ready for this meeting with Mrs. Z with the keen understanding and true belief that I only had to be responsible for my own behavior—and that *only* I could consent and award her the power to upset me. The direction of the meeting was in my control and I only had to control my own behaviors. If Mrs. Z was angry or once again deeply disappointed in our work with her children, then *she* owned that behavior, not me. I needn't feel guilty or upset or take her comments personally. I felt much more confident of my skills and felt in control of my emotions.

Learn to Listen Attentively

Being an introvert, I was nearly always overwhelmed by Mrs. Z's tirades. I couldn't think fast enough on my feet to respond to her. I too often let her speak without limits while I searched for the perfect words, answers, or solutions, only to discover them on the tip of my tongue hours or even days later. In past encounters, anything was, or could be, fair game. I never knew where the conversations would take us and therefore was unable to prepare and rehearse in the fashion that the introvert in me prefers. Compound this with the fact that Mrs. Z did not appear to respect my position and that I did not trust her. Clearly, there was little opportunity for honest and open communications between us. Yet, for the sake of her children, and for my sanity, I wanted to develop better communications and a more positive working relationship.

David Sanderson's materials once again proved to be very helpful to me. During my fall graduate course, I had reviewed David's handout, "The Attentive Leader, Drawing Others Out," paying close attention to five communication skills that would benefit me in my work with my graduate project team. These skills—paying attention, listening for the whole message, hearing before evaluating (a recognized priority for me), reflecting or paraphrasing, and summarizing—were recognized as important elements in my communications with Mrs. Z, other parents, and colleagues.

I also gave a lot of thought to ineffective listening behaviors during this review, and I found myself easily identifying with several of them. One such behavior is rehearsing—getting ready to respond while another person is talking. Here I am guilty as charged. I honestly attribute this behavior to the emerging understanding of myself as an introvert. I often feel uncomfortable thinking on my feet and use rehearsal as a strategy to assist me in being both more comfortable and more effective when communicating. I may then find myself rehearsing a response that is not needed, or would not be needed had I listened more carefully. David Sanderson also lists the ineffective habit of analyzing possible motives while listening. There are times that I will analyze for days why Mrs. Z wants to meet with me and then spend hours considering her motives. After we meet, I may find that my analysis was entirely off base and I had worried for naught.

Covey (1990) addresses the goal, "Seek first to understand, then be understood" (p. 237). This goal also has a significant meaning for me. As stated above, I have the habit of formulating my responses as someone is speaking. I do not listen to understand. Rather, I listen with the intent to reply. I listen within my own biographical framework and may find myself commenting, "Yes, I've been through that. I understand completely. I know what you've been going through." I may even share my own stories, often of doom and gloom.

This limits my ability to be an empathic listener. Covey views empathic listening as the highest form of listening. It is listening to understand, allowing you to get inside another person's frame of reference. With empathic listening, you are more able to "fully, deeply, understand that person, emotionally as well as intellectually" (Covey, 1990, p. 240). If I ask the questions, "Do I utilize empathic listening skills when meeting with Mrs. Z? Do I understand Mrs. Z's point of view? Where she is coming from?" I must honestly answer, "No." What, then, could I do to improve the effectiveness of our communications?

Meeting With Mrs. Z

I spent some time after the January 11, 1993, Writers' Collaborative meeting reflecting on how well the group was functioning and on how well all of the MASL groups I have participated in have functioned. The common thread for me was the time we have taken in these groups to establish ground rules for guiding our meetings. What I felt was missing in my meetings with Mrs. Z were ground rules or, as I view them, guidelines both to set the tone and to provide me with some much needed direction.

I then set forth to develop a list of guidelines to present to Mrs. Z in writing when I met with her. In doing so I recognized a major limitation with this effort. Unlike our MASL groups or Writers' Collaborative, Mrs. Z was not involved in drafting these guidelines and therefore had no stake in using them or upholding them. Would she be offended by my attempts to focus our meeting? It was a new addition to our interactions and might create additional conflict, but I was prepared to take the risk and face the conflict if it came.

So, on the morning of January 14, I met with Mrs. Z. It was essential that I set a positive tone for the meeting, and I had prepared for this by having ground rules ready at the outset of our meeting. I had also rehearsed my opening. I began.

"Mrs. Z. When you called to schedule this meeting, you told me that you had a number of concerns about your son that needed to be addressed. Before we discuss your concerns, I would like to suggest four guidelines to help us focus our discussion today."

I then shared the written list of guidelines with her. These were limited to four points, with the beginning and ending statements purposefully written to be both positive and collaborative in nature. I was sure that Mrs. Z, or any parent for that matter, would strongly agree that she did share high expectations for her son and that she wanted him to be both happy and successful in the classroom. I continued by reading the guidelines.

"I know that we can agree that we both share high expectations for your son. This includes high expectations for both his behavior and his work in the classroom. We need to focus today's meeting on what your current concerns are. We will also limit our discussion to concerns for your son, and not other parents' concerns that you might be aware of."

Mrs. Z seemed to be very receptive to the guidelines and I continued with the final point.

"I know that we both want your son to be happier in his classroom, to be challenged, and to feel successful. I am sure that we both share these goals, and I am eager to work together with you to develop some workable solutions."

By presenting the guidelines in writing before we started our discussions, I was successful in my goal of setting a defined and positive focus. I was pleased that Mrs. Z was receptive to the written guidelines. We began by having her share her child's concerns and any problems she perceived in the classroom, and I made my best attempt to employ effective listening skills. I paraphrased her concerns to be certain that I understood them clearly and was interpreting them correctly, then asked her to share her own concerns. These, too, were paraphrased before I voiced the concerns shared by the child's classroom teacher and me.

The tone throughout remained focused, cordial, and calm. When we had each aired what we viewed as problems, I addressed the need to solicit additional information. I proposed a series of classroom observations over a 2-week period that would enable me to document her son's behavior and work in the classroom as well as the classroom teacher's responses to these. We agreed to meet after the observations were completed in order to discuss the results and address the concerns in light of the results. We also agreed at that time to discuss and develop collaboratively solutions that would enable her son to reach the goal of being happier and more successful in the classroom setting.

I had also prepared well by reviewing her son's records carefully. I was thus able to keep our discussion focused on her child's learning successes and challenges and how these were impacting his work in Grade 6. The focus remained on her son and his needs and not on the inadequacies of my colleagues, as had been the pattern in the past. The meeting ended on a friendly tone and was the briefest I have had with her in 4 years. Even my secretary was surprised to see Mrs. Z emerge from my office after only 20 minutes. She was perhaps even more surprised to see me follow Mrs. Z with a light step, offering a cordial thank you and farewell.

Continuing to Learn

This was not my last conference with Mrs. Z, though I view it as a turning point in what had been a very difficult parent-school relationship in the past. Our meeting in February to review the results of the classroom observations and outline our expectations for her son was very positive and collaborative in nature. We met again in April to discuss a behavior episode with her son. Past discussions of this nature had been volatile, but during this one we both remained calm and focused on her son's behaviors, and I left the meeting feeling confident and sure of my decisions.

I didn't even lose my cool, or my confidence, when she came flying into my office one Monday morning in June, stating that she was angry at the school and fed up with things. After a heated exchange, she left my office slamming the door. My staff, most of whom witnessed her loud accusations from the teachers' room, was surprised to see me leave my office looking controlled, quite calm, and nearly stress free. In fact, in many ways I felt energized and proud of myself for keeping my focus and controlling my emotions. What a difference in my behaviors and skills in working with this parent from previous encounters over the past 5 years! In many ways I view the January 14 meeting as the beginning of a new relationship with this very difficult parent. It is a slow process but one that will undoubtedly benefit me, Mrs. Z, and her children in some very important ways.

These professional development opportunities have guided me through a process of self-reflection. In this process I have learned much about my personality traits, about how I deal (or don't deal) with conflict, and how my behaviors impact my relationships with family, friends, colleagues, and parents. I am recognizing how many small events and encounters that would have previously gone unnoticed impact my life in new and subtle ways. Two years ago I would never have considered Mrs. Z to be a likely resource in my journey of self-reflection. I have discovered that even the Mrs. Zs in my life may play integral roles in my quest for personal and professional change. For these lessons, I thank her.

Reference

Covey, S. (1990). *The seven habits of highly effective people: Restoring the character ethic.* New York: Simon & Schuster.

SURPRISING OUTCOMES
Or
Why *Do* They Read Macbeth?

A high school teacher becomes the chair of her English Department and learns to balance ambition and colleagueship.

Elizabeth Wiley

Four years ago, the English department was a fairly comfortable place. We knew all the rules—we were the good guys, our critics were the bad guys, the principal was a coward—and we spent our department meetings rephrasing those rules with the style, grace, and nuance (heavy on the nuance) that only English teachers can exercise in the late afternoon.

We had reason to feel besieged. People had often chosen to move to our community because the schools were good, and generally they'd been satisfied, or at least they'd been quiet about their dissatisfaction. In the past years, though, as our reputation climbed higher and higher (a phenomenon tied to the introduction of statewide testing), people seemed to feel duped. If we were the best in the state, why weren't their children learning more? Why couldn't they read and write better? And why, oh why, weren't their SAT scores higher? They called us lazy and inept. We called them overambitious and naive. Of course, because the two camps never talked to each other, all of this name-calling stayed sub rosa and we were able to be woodenly polite at soccer games and awards banquets.

Then we found a common enemy in our new principal. He was a good man with very good intentions—in fact, he was primarily responsible for most of the positive changes that happened, sometimes painfully, over the next few years—but he offended as many people as he pleased. It wasn't intentional; he simply lacked grace in dealing with people. His enthusiasm was seen as insensitivity; his candor, as arrogance. I've spent months wondering where his administration went wrong, and that's as close as I can get to the source of the trouble.

However complex the reasons, our initial reactions to the principal were based on simple things. We disliked him because he was in charge when the school board increased the English teacher load from four classes to five. Parents disliked him because he couldn't "schmooze." We assured each other that he was the trouble and did nothing more.

But then he moved into our territory. It's hard for me to stay mad at him here because he was rushing to my defense at the time, so I'll try to tell the story without embellishment. Historically, the chair of the English department has allotted course divisions after consulting with teachers. It's not very complicated; we all have our specialties and we usually teach pretty much the same load from year to year. The difficulty comes when a particularly large class moves through and adjustments must be made to the standard pattern.

It was June and the courses had been allotted. The switch from four to five classes was scheduled for the next year and the principal was making conciliatory visits to each of us before we disappeared for the summer. He told me that it was his hope that we could each keep the same number of students spread over five classes so that, although we'd have more preparations, we'd have no more papers to grade. I told him that my load was way up from 80 (our school board has really tried to limit our student load to 80, which is one of several reasons I like teaching here).

He checked the figures. It turned out that the chair of the English department was teaching three junior classes and two study skills

courses for a total of 66 students. I had three senior classes and two
freshman for a total of 110. I know that teachers too often get bogged
down in comparing workloads, but I also know that teachers don't
husband their energy, giving out less to each student when there are
more of them in a class. We worry about each student, we plan lessons for individual interests, we call parents when we need information. We don't worry, plan, or call less when there are more students;
we try to stretch our energies to cover them all. I was not looking
forward to that much stretching.

Because I was on vacation and taking a course, what happened
next is hazy to me. I've heard two versions, but because there are almost no points of agreement between the two I'll cut to the result. In
September, I was teaching three senior classes, the chair had three junior classes and we each had one freshman class and one study skills
course. And she had resigned as chair of the department.

It was an awful year. First, we had no chair. Then the principal
was going to chair our meetings. Then he asked us all to chair them
jointly. Then our old chair was back, but our meetings were still devoted to licking our wounds. We didn't even do the ritualistic department bookkeeping (cleverly designed to keep us off awkward subjects
like "What are we doing and why?") By May, most of the department
still wasn't speaking to the principal and the chair had found a job in
New Hampshire for the following year. You'd think that we would all
be filing transfers to the math department, but when they asked for
applications for the position as chair, three of the five of us applied.

Can I Make a Difference?

I don't know why I got the job, except that I was the only appli-
cant who hadn't chaired a department before and they were relying
on beginner's luck. I don't even know why I wanted it so badly. I love
teaching and I was learning more about it every day. Shifting my focus to being department chair might slow that down. But I was frustrated with going it alone and I thought I could help the department
make a collective impact on kids. It seemed that I alone could do very
little to affect my students' learning; they came to me from the void
and disappeared into it again. Oh, I knew that they read *Romeo and
Juliet* as freshmen and *Macbeth* as seniors, but I hadn't any idea what

they were supposed to *know* when they came to me—or, for that matter, what they were supposed to know when they left. It was safer to teach them everything I could. Maybe, if I could use my role as chair to get us to talk, the other English teachers would drop some hints.

I had come into education in my mid-thirties, recruited into an experimental program to certify teachers who had had other careers. We, the other interns and I, had felt our way tentatively through our training and internships, learning the complicated ways of schools and making sense of them only through hours of discussion. Those discussions had supported, excited, and galvanized me through my first few years in the classroom. Maybe that's what I hoped to recapture in department meetings. I didn't hope for big changes quickly, though. My goal was to discuss the teaching of English by the following spring. We almost made it.

That first year I led by example. I was collegial, friendly, and collaborative with my fellow teachers. I gave them fliers for conferences and urged them to go. I passed out mailings from the Foxfire Network and the Coalition for Essential Schools and coaxed them into discussing them. I wrote up agendas that focused on authentic assessment and heterogeneous grouping. Upon reflection, I was arrogant, presumptuous, and rude. These were all experienced teachers—much more experienced than I—and I presumed to tell them, through my not-so-subtle messages, that they needed to improve and that I knew exactly what form that improvement should take.

The summer after my first year as chair—the summer of '92— several forces came together serendipitously to show me how wrong I had been: I read Stephen Covey's *Seven Habits of Highly Effective People* (1990), went to the MASL summer institute, and spent 9 days at a national conference on assessment run by some of the guiding lights of the reform movement. The last was particularly enlightening: They preached with a holier-than-thou tone that I found repulsive, yet familiar. Then I realized that that was what I must have sounded like to my colleagues in the English department.

I knew that I had been treating them badly, but treating them well couldn't mean going back to the status quo where we were all independent operators blaming any shortcomings on the kids or on the system. I still didn't know why my students read *Macbeth* or what I was expected to teach them; I couldn't even guarantee that they had

really learned what I had taught. That's where the outcomes grant
came in.

One Success Can Lead To Another . . .

In 1989 we had been given a $25,000 grant through the Coalition
of Essential Schools to write outcomes in every subject. The rest of the
school had at least started on this task, but our department hadn't. I
had reminded the members of the department regularly—probably
in that same whining tone that makes me flinch now to remember—
but they'd managed to shrug me off.

I had a long talk with myself—several, in fact—and because I walk
when I talk, I was in great shape when fall rolled around. By then I
had decided what mattered to me: that we had a good set of working
outcomes by November, that we spend the rest of the year evaluating
them, and that we begin working together as a team for the benefit of
the students. So, in the best interests of everyone, I told a little lie.

Actually, it was more of a manipulation of the truth. I knew that
the school board was interested in the progress of the outcomes and
that the department would be more likely to work on them if they
knew that the board was watching, so I called the superintendent and
asked when she'd like the department to report to the board. She liked
the idea so much that she put together a whole language arts presentation—K-12—and scheduled it for November.

At the end of August, I wrote to the members of the department
telling them of the reporting deadline and informing them that we'd
need to meet twice a month to get ready. I also told them that I knew
that collectively we knew everything we needed to know to write
outcomes that would work in the best interests of our students; we
would be our own experts, our own consultants, because there weren't
any better ones around. And I meant it.

They were wonderful—once they were convinced that I truly val-
ued their expertise. We started with outcomes in writing research papers, partly because they were the least personal, partly because our
wonderful librarian was eager to help. Most of us knew that we needed
to teach our students how to write research papers, but none of us
had ever developed the same careful lessons and units in this area
that we had in reading, writing, and speech (the other outcome areas). In fact, with the exception of one teacher of American literature,

most of us had hurried through research papers, remembering—and probably duplicating—our own unpleasant high school experiences.

We started with the Coalition injunction to plan backwards. What did we want seniors to be able to do in research by the time they left us? We envisioned self-motivated researchers, designing their own projects and presenting them to a panel of critics (why not dream big?). With some form of that as an end product, we worked backwards to the junior project, a lengthy paper that incorporated primary sources and was marked by a student-designed, original thesis. The sophomore paper would ask students to compare two systems—of belief, social order, mythology, whatever. The freshman research would be modeled on Ken McCrory's I-Search paper, a process that starts in a student's own expertise and pushes it into new territory.

When we were done, we not only had a design for challenging research outcomes and systems for helping students to meet those challenges, we had a model for working together that was both effective and pleasant. From there on, nothing could stop us. We sailed through those outcomes, arguing over sequence and wrestling with details, but working together. By November, we not only had a good working set of outcomes, we owned them.

Expect the Best, and Get It

Somewhere along the way, I had learned more about leadership than any workshop, any self-help book, or any lecture could ever teach. In describing others as whiny and self-centered, I'd only been describing myself. When I learned to honor my colleagues as professionals, they treated me professionally. It felt almost like magic, but it shouldn't have: We know that students reflect the expectations that adults have for them. And, as any teacher knows, most classroom lessons are metaphors for the rest of life.

Department meetings are still contentious, but now we're wrestling with bigger questions: How much *can* a department work together without inhibiting the creativity of individual members? Is teaching—as one colleague claims—an ephemeral art that can't be taught? If it is, how do we ever guarantee that students learn what they need to know? Where does community opinion come in? Should parents be consulted on major curriculum issues? Course assignments? And which parents?

I wanted to become chair because I wanted to provide leadership for the department; now I find myself looking for a higher vision of leadership—not from the principal or the superintendent; they've both been wonderful—but from the community, as interpreted by the school board. The greatest achievement of my tenure—the outcomes—came because we had a clear sense of what the community expected of us and what it wanted for its children. The most painful moments—arguments over standards, politics surrounding teaching assignments—came when the community was clearly ambivalent.

I'm not asking the board to take sides on all these issues but to continue to formulate a vision for the school that becomes paramount, that supersedes any squabbles, and that provides a touchstone for those of us who have to make the thousands of little decisions that cumulatively create a school. A good starting point would be for all of us to treat everyone involved in schools—staff, students, parents, community—with honor and dignity. It has worked for us in our department. I know it would work for our schools.

Reference

Covey, S. (1990). *The seven habits of highly effective people: Restoring the character ethic.* New York: Simon & Schuster.

FROM I TO WE:
A Middle School Story

A first year principal cuts his teeth as a leader by building disparate teachers into a middle level team.

Patrick R. Phillips

I'm finished now with my first year as principal of a K-8 school in a small Maine town. It has been the most remarkable year of my career, full of personal and professional challenge, a healthy measure of conflict resolution, and a few qualified successes. The Maine Academy for School Leaders prepared me—as well as any program could—for the tribulations of the principalship. And yet, when I look back on the discrepancy between what I expected and what I have experienced, the gap is considerable.

My experience in the Academy introduced into my understanding of school leadership several beliefs that I have attempted to apply in my current position: that a school can move toward functioning as a community of learners; that the whole school should be reflected in our vision of school improvement; that efforts to improve school programs must take into account the complex intra- and interpersonal dimensions of school culture; and that if I am to succeed—or even survive—as a school leader I must continue to develop a deeper understanding of how my personality is manifested in certain strengths and weaknesses that bear directly on my work as a principal.

Did these beliefs serve me well? Do I still believe them? In the following pages, I take stock of myself and my leadership convictions. I review the major events in our schoolwide planning over the year, reflect on our middle school as a test case for the above beliefs, and look back on my thoughts and feelings during this most intense year of my life. Each of these aspects relates to the I-C-I model we used in the Academy: The whole school context equates with the program or Cognitive level; the middle school, the Interpersonal; and my own reflections, the Intrapersonal. These observations will run together through a chronology of events beginning in the late summer of 1993 and concluding in early summer of the following year.

August-October

When I took the job as principal last summer, one school board member reportedly said that he supported my candidacy because he saw me as an "educational leader." Whether his perception of my abilities was warranted remains an open question, but his comment does reflect the general expectation that the school was ready for, if not in need of, some direction. The board had voted the last 2 years for including a once-a-month, half day of release time in the school calendar to promote staff research and restructuring. No significant recommendations were put forward in the first year except to continue to study several promising areas: multiaging in the primary grades, middle school reform, and computer technology.

Early in the fall, I spoke with the staff about the need for us to apply a rigorous approach to completing our research on these topics and making recommendations to the board in the spring. With this general expectation, we divided up into "focus groups," which were to meet on our half days in each of the areas noted above. The multiage primary and computer groups got off to great starts and continued during the year to conduct highly productive conversations that yielded sharply focused recommendations. The middle school group also came to closure on several recommendations, but the philosophical and interpersonal differences among the middle school staff made getting to closure something of a hair-raising experience.

The middle school is defined in our building as Grades 6 through 8. We have two classes at each level and the six teachers at the time were divided rather neatly into two groups—three who favored restructuring along the lines of recent middle school research (the "middle-schoolers"), and three who were less inclined to alter their more traditional approach ("status quo" group). All six were intelligent and committed teachers whose philosophical and personal differences had become rather hardened in recent years. (I should add that I have oversimplified these distinctions for purposes of casting the story in sharper relief. These broad strokes have no doubt done injustice to all points of view described herein.)

I learned that my predecessor had attempted to move the middle school toward reform by means of direct administrative pressure, but her efforts had ultimately been unsuccessful and in the end she had left the problem to me. At the first meeting of our middle school focus group—full of high hopes and a degree of bravado—I said that I expected us to prepare a set of recommendations for presentation to the board in the spring. There was the goal (it seemed simple enough to me) but from the tight-lipped expressions around me, I surmised that my optimism about coming to consensus was not widely shared.

In the coming weeks, the depth of the personal and philosophical differences among the middle school staff became clear to me. The atmosphere over the past several years had become contaminated with suspicion, anger, and frustration. In order to facilitate a more constructive dialogue among the middle school staff, I spent numerous hours arranging for a graduate-level course on middle school theory to be held at our school. The three middle-schoolers enrolled right away, even though each had already taken such a course within the last 4 years. Each of the more traditional teachers cited very compelling reasons for not being able to join in.

At first, this declaration of noninvolvement left me discouraged and wondering whether the teachers who had become rather chronically discouraged were right. But after three or four other teachers in the building enrolled in the course, including two specialists and the two fifth-grade teachers, I began to see the outlines of a strategy to create a temporary—but perhaps false—majority by broadening the decision-making process to include these other teachers. This ran the risk of deepening the divisions already polarizing the middle school, but I saw no other way to avoid paralysis. It was also a step in the direction of building a whole school context for school improvement discussions.

At the same time, I felt that I must do something to ease some of the interpersonal tensions in the school. My first effort was to encourage one of the status quo group to accept the role of team leader of the middle school. The board had recently approved the practice of rotating the role of team leader on a yearly basis, and her name was first in the order of rotation. She had the right to pass, and many expected her to defer to the next person in line, a highly committed member of the middle-schoolers group. In encouraging the veteran teacher to accept the position, I wondered whether the reform-minded teachers in the middle school and elsewhere in the building might misinterpret my support, but I thought of it as an opportunity to involve her more deeply in the decision-making process and thought the risks were warranted. Because the numbers—as they had been stacked—would favor moving us toward my goal of a more constructive dialogue, I believed that it was extremely important to cultivate positive working relationships with members of the status quo group.

On a more personal level, I had the sense that the faculty was watching me very closely, that each of my actions or statements carried great significance. Early days on the job found me swamped in soul-searching. What concrete things *could* I do to move a school with a history of internal discord toward becoming a community of learners? I had been very impressed with the influence that Roland Barth brought to the Academy. On the surface, his idea of a school where adults and kids are primarily committed to learning seemed simple enough, though the more I thought about it, the more I recognized the countless obstacles in getting there. Would my modeling such a commitment, showing myself to be the "head learner," be enough? With this group, I was not so sure.

I remember having the feeling that I was out of my depth, but that if I could just give the appearance of knowing what I was doing for a while, maybe I could learn enough to eventually achieve a more solid footing. Being an unknown quantity was a terrific blessing, as it gave me a chance to assert some parts of my personality that I had not been in a position to reveal before. However, I was not at all confident about my chances for success. Fortunately for me, the staff had developed a very accepting and hopeful attitude about me—something akin to the honeymoon phenomenon—and was very supportive of my initial efforts.

November-January

During the fall and early winter, the very enthusiastic middle-school-course group continued to develop a stronger commitment to reform. The focus group, on the other hand, suffered during its monthly meetings from the polarizing effect of the deep personal and philosophical divisions among the six middle school classroom teachers. This was apparently more pronounced when I was not in attendance. I was told by the chairperson of the focus group, a middle-schooler, that the typical sequence of events at a meeting would be that a reform question or topic would be placed before the group for discussion, followed by a spirited conversation on the topic which would end with no resolution having been reached and tensions reinforced. This pattern, and the fact that it happened more when I was not around, had deepened the sense of discouragement felt by the chairperson and others who hoped to see some agreement reached.

For my own part, I was beginning to feel that the problems were too deeply ingrained for me to have any effect. My early sense of optimism and euphoria at being hired as a principal was giving way to a growing sense of dread that the middle school tensions would spill over into the rest of the school. As my uncertainty with the middle school team intensified, I began looking for some more effective way of using a larger context as a stimulus for change.

In my previous work, I had experienced firsthand how a school can get so fragmented that good practices and successes are overshadowed. So I was committed to looking for opportunities to get the staff to see the benefits of a "whole-school" approach. I had come to think of myself as a person capable of synthesizing and articulating ideas rather well. The Myers-Briggs work we had done at the Academy helped me to see this as a strength. My type, INTP, typically enjoys creating the "architecture" of systems. Perhaps I could use this ability to help the staff identify and commit to shared goals.

The school board and superintendent had been open to my suggestion of revisiting our school philosophy, beginning with our fundamental beliefs, and basing any recommendations for changed practice on these essential commitments. I was given the authority to assemble a broad-based committee of parents, board members, teachers, students, and community members to identify and express a set of common beliefs and expectations for our school. The committee took up its work in late October, with the stated goal of having a new philosophy ready for board approval in late winter. My greatest fear at this point was that these various discussions—the focus groups, the middle school course, the philosophy committee—would all go off in separate directions. I had a sense of where I would like us to go based on my own beliefs, but I wondered just how much consensus there was among the staff, board, and community.

Because looking at my own type and analyzing how types affect group dynamics had been helpful to me during the Academy, I decided that if I could find the means, I would have the staff take the Myers-Briggs inventory as well. I was pretty certain that the staff was aware of how smoldering interpersonal conflicts could have a destructive influence in a school, but I was unclear just how willing people would be to accept a new set of ideas as a way of healing old wounds. I called around to find a consultant who could both give us an introduction to the Myers-Briggs and help us reach consensus on areas of common practice. In retrospect, this turned out to be one of the best decisions I made all year.

The consultant and I met to lay plans for her visit with us on an inservice day in mid-January. We agreed that prior to her coming I would solicit a set of belief statements from the staff to serve as a starting point for our discussion. The staff turned in their basic belief statements to me and I wrote them on construction paper, which I displayed at a holiday gathering for the school staff. These statements, when viewed together, had a powerful effect: It was clear that the vast majority of the faculty—whether primary, intermediate, or middle school—shared a common set of core beliefs about the importance of focusing on the whole child, establishing a positive school climate, setting high expectations for learning across an interdisciplinary curriculum, seeking richer ways to assess student progress, building teamwork structures to promote adult learning, and increasing parent and community involvement in the school.

When we returned from the holiday break, I transferred the staff beliefs into a written document and circulated it for comment. I also shared it with the committee working on the new philosophy statement, and it was immediately observed that the staff's belief statements paralleled the work the committee had produced to date. Thus, by the mid-January inservice day, the rough outline of a set of shared beliefs was beginning to take shape.

However, to many of the faculty, the picture of where we were heading with all of this was not coming into sharp focus rapidly enough. Several faculty expressed their frustrations to me that we had too many irons in the fire: a philosophy committee, several focus groups, and an upcoming inservice day on the Myers-Briggs framework. In short, people felt overwhelmed. I was beginning to feel nervous that my INTP, "architect-of-systems" personality type was really not at all capable of getting down to the concrete level required to make relevant decisions in a school context. Was I off on a meaningless tangent? Were people beginning to lose confidence in my ability to bring us together? These thoughts did their best to displace my sense of satisfaction at our shared beliefs.

I can remember thinking at the beginning of our January inservice day that much was riding on the outcome of the day's work. We would either have taken a step toward understanding and healing some of the staff's interpersonal wounds or deepened the divisions within our group. We would either have clarified and solidified our common beliefs or cast in sharper detail our philosophical differences. As it happened, our consultant did a marvelous job of treating the Myers-Briggs presentation with the right balance of lightheartedness and meaning. Though several staff were vocal in their disapproval of such techniques, on the whole, people took it as it was presented: one framework among many that can produce insights into human relations. One staff member said, after our general discussion, that she felt a sense of not only understanding but forgiveness about what people had done or said in the past.

By the end of our discussion, an important milestone had been reached: The staff had attained just enough breathing room to be able to dislodge some of the entrenched notions that kept them from seeing each other in an accepting light. We were not able to take up the Myers-Briggs in great detail, but we did learn enough about it to look at ourselves and each other with a bit more grace and humor. In the scheme of things, that proved to be enough. One minor note emerged from our analysis: When I displayed the types present among the staff on a 16-cell matrix, I was the only one out of a 25-person staff in the entire right hand column (the NT temperament). Would this prove to be a complementary distribution, with me adding certain characteristics not otherwise present in the school? Or would this represent an unbridgable gap between me and my faculty?

As for our shared beliefs, by the end of the inservice day we had taken the rough outline created before the holidays, discussed it in greater detail, compared it to the work of the philosophy committee, and recognized for the record that there was indeed a significant degree of agreement, a critical mass, if you will. I can remember among us an almost palpable sense of shared pride and an anticipation of building on these beliefs. For my own part, I knew that the next steps would be easier now, though far from certain. Momentum was building.

February-June

By early February, the philosophy committee had completed a draft statement to be submitted for approval by the board. The draft philosophy statement and the faculty's common beliefs turned out to be very similar and, in the final stages, each had influenced the other. The philosophy adopted by the board in February was not a radical document, but it did clarify our school's commitment to a positive school climate, interdisciplinary instruction, authentic learning, alternative assessment, teacher collaboration, and community involvement. The logical next step for the school as a whole—and the middle school in particular—was to take this framework and establish focused goals in each area for the coming year. For the primary and intermediate divisions, this was a relatively straightforward task; for the middle school, however, a number of obstacles had to be surmounted first.

Painted in broad strokes, the middle school staff faced the tasks of agreeing on concrete actions for the next school year and reaching a level of interpersonal acceptance within the team that allowed them to work more comfortably and effectively together. In order to reinforce the idea that action steps or goals for the coming year were to be developed within a whole-school context, I created a large-scale matrix (roughly 4' x 8') with the broad categories from our philosophy and belief statements listed on one axis and each of the teams (K-2, 3-5, 6-8, and specialists) on the other. The staff and I had joked during the year about my tendency to reduce every discussion to a series of boxes, but on this occasion everyone agreed that an organized representation of our plans would be beneficial.

I was painfully aware of what a critical point this was for the middle school team (and for me as well!). Would the increasingly whole-school consensus be enough to break the impasse? Would the somewhat contrived majority of the middle school focus group enable decisions to be made and carried out by the smaller, more divided middle school staff? Would our initial groundwork in the Myers-Briggs framework enable us to reduce the tensions enough to communicate more openly?

The matter of setting middle school goals for the coming year was taken up by the focus group which was, as noted, chaired by one of the middle-schoolers. I made a point of encouraging the teams to set realistic goals, to avoid taking on more than could be effectively accomplished. To help reassure those who were less than enthusiastic about changed practice, I also made it clear that within our goals, whatever they might be, there would be room for differences of style, emphasis, and commitment level.

The chairperson had done her usual thorough job of preparing for the goal-setting session and had listed options for the team to consider within each of the categories of the philosophy statement. Like a safecracker hearing tumblers fall into place, I listened to the discussion with silent satisfaction. The team identified three major goals with little or no dissent: The middle school would institute an advisor/advisee program, commit as a group to portfolio assessment and student-parent-teacher conferences, and make the math program less ability grouped. When the results of this and the other team discussions were recorded on our large-scale matrix, it was clear that there would indeed be a whole-school set of goals. The context had been set and the middle school had formally agreed to program changes. However, the interpersonal dimension had yet to be completely dealt with.

Now that we had reached some agreements, I asked the staff during our next workday to reflect on the process we had used to date. For the most part, the staff expressed satisfaction at both the process and the product (our goals) and pride that we had gotten so much done. But then, the bombshell: One of the veteran middle school teachers gave an impassioned speech on his disagreement with our basic assumptions about the need for change. He pointed out that our school had scored very well in the 8th-grade state standardized tests the previous year and concluded by claiming that many of us were "changing for change's sake." In the uncomfortable silence that followed a few people applauded, but I suspected that most were wondering whether this was the opening salvo in a larger, more divisive struggle.

Though I did respond with a few comments about our decisions being based on research and study, I chose not to confront the person or the attitude that may have been shared by a few others. I thought of the moment as a real test of our general health as a staff. Could such a statement be uttered and taken for what it was—one person's point of view? Would the majority of the staff feel secure enough in their commitments to listen to disagreements without getting into some kind of informal, behind-the-scenes trench warfare? Would the reformers on the staff demand that I counter the statement with one of equal intensity? And finally, would the middle school staff now retreat from their consensus into the perfectly balanced, three-versus-three deadlock?

For me, the statement did produce some degree of uncertainty about the relative weight of my efforts up to then. I questioned again my assumptions about the importance of context and setting a vision for a school. What good was an "architect of systems" if the person could not also get the structure built? I also worried that my attempt to move us toward greater understanding and appreciation of individual differences was merely a drop in the bucket compared to the divisions that had prevented closer working relationships from developing in the past.

The statement did send a shock wave through the middle school reform discussion. Two of the middle-schoolers came to me to express concerns about the interpersonal tensions that still made any team conversation about goals for the next year strained and inconclusive. It was clear that we needed a middle school team meeting to clear the air. When the team got together, several days hence, I described my role as facilitator of a discussion about the interpersonal dimension of teamwork and decision making. I reminded the staff about the Myers-Briggs work we had done and reiterated my commitment to looking for ways to build on people's strengths.

In the end, two things happened at the meeting that allowed us to move ahead. First, the team leader, speaking I believe on behalf of the other members of the status quo group, reassured everyone that the team's goals were indeed common and that everyone would be working on implementing them. She argued, however, that there was room within the goals for people to find their own comfort level. Her acknowledgment that the decisions we had reached were not being questioned allowed, I think, a second breakthrough to occur: Team members remarked to one another that they had made assumptions about each other that had polarized the group.

It seemed at the time like a small step, but it had the immediate effect of reassuring the middle-schoolers that we could in fact make progressive change while enabling the status quo group to feel they would be heard and shape the process. Like all good compromises, everyone got something and everyone gave ground.

The feeling at the end of the meeting made me reconsider the effect of the "change for change's sake" statement: Rather than being an opening salvo for a new round of conflict, it seemed in retrospect to be something final, a parting shot at the end of an era.

The middle school story had reached and passed the point of climax. In the following weeks, I translated our school goals into a written report that took elements from all our work during the year. In it were belief statements from the teachers, language from our new philosophy, background narrative from me, and our team goals described in the context of whole-school commitments. Frankly, I was shocked at the overwhelmingly positive response to the report. Many members of the faculty saw this polished document as an indication of the professionalism displayed during the decision-making process; in short, they were proud. The report was submitted to the board by the team leader, excerpted for the parents, and shared with other schools. It symbolized, I believe, collective commitment to something larger than oneself; the whole-school context gave meaning to the hard work and compromise.

The second event was smaller in scale but equally symbolic to me. One of the status quo group had agreed during the third quarter to join one of the middle-schoolers in a portfolio student-parent-teacher conference project. The conferences had gone very well. Students had accomplished masses of terrific work to share with their parents and had spoken clearly and analytically about their work. Parents had raved. Unexpectedly, the status quo teacher stopped by the office after the conferences had ended and enthusiastically praised the results. I told him I was glad he enjoyed the portfolio conferences and looked

forward to seeing the process developed further next year. It was
deeply gratifying for me to sense his excitement, and ; represented to
me that change is an odd collection of events, some predictable and
some surprising.

The final event was a meeting of the middle school staff to plan
our summer's work. Several staff members were planning to attend
the middle school institute at the University of Maine. Their task was
to make specific plans for how our advisor/advisee program would
work. In addition, two teachers and I agreed to assemble a guide to
portfolio assessment that would help us start the year with a common
knowledge base. But the work assignments were less important to me
than the clear sense of teamwork that was present. I suspect that no
one there would have predicted at the outset that we could end the
year as a team, but there we were, making plans for sharing the
workload and implementing our goals.

Summer Reflections

Looking back from the relative peace and calm of early July, I
wonder what insights I should take from the year just passed. Am I
correct in thinking that the whole-school context for change enabled
us to overcome inertia? Did the Myers-Briggs work create just enough
breathing room for people to see each other in a more accepting light?
A neutral observer might point to any number of alternative explana-
tions for the progress we made (honeymoon period, negotiations not
going on, one step forward before two steps back, etc.). In the end, I
am probably too close to the situation to bring much objectivity to it.
But this reflection is really more about subjective truth anyway—what
it all means to me as the principal of this school.

From that intrapersonal perspective, my experiences this year have
indeed strengthened my commitment to see the school as a community of learners, seek a whole-school context for change, build deeper
understanding of the intra- and interpersonal dimensions of school
culture, and create opportunities for myself and others to reflect on
our lives as educators. That final commitment may be the most significant, for now that I have gotten my thoughts about the year out on
paper, I am struck by the difficulty of unraveling the complex tangle
of events I have just lived through. Without some regular, honest, and

perhaps shared opportunities to step back from the dizzying pace of the daily life of a school, acquiring any sense of context or meaning is all but impossible.

I began this reflection with the observation that a large discrepancy exists between what I expected as a first-year principal and what I experienced. The one gift from the Academy that made the gap more comprehensible is the perspective that schools—like any purposeful collection of humans—are multidimensional and vastly more difficult to understand or change than we expect. That anything substantive happened this year is rather miraculous, and I am grateful and proud that it did. Did my efforts make a difference? I hope so.

LIVING WITH AMBIGUITY:
The Promise and Perils of
Teacher Leadership

A teacher shares excerpts from her journal of attempts to provide informal leadership for her school's innovative agenda.

Sally Mackenzie

I am a high school teacher. Until this year, I never had time to keep a journal. But I decided in September 1993 to do so because I was part of the Writers' Collaborative. I produced something every month so that my fellow writers/practitioners could help me make sense of my experience as a teacher leader. My journal shows the kinds of risks I took this year in trying to bring my school and colleagues to a greater understanding of accountability for themselves and their students.

I triumphed in some ways, although there were numerous tribulations. In the end, the question I faced was "Is it worth it to seek to change my school?" My ambivalence about the vulnerability—not to mention sheer work—involved might give others pause to think as they embark on the murky path of teacher leadership.

Stepping Into a Vacuum

The year had started out so well. I had several leadership roles in the school as lead teacher, coordinator of an action research project in reading and writing assessment, and staff developer. Furthermore, a teacher who had been instrumental in planning for change through the "diploma project," our school's plan for student accountability structured on competency-based outcomes, had left to get a doctorate. There was a power vacuum, and I filled it, albeit very differently from the way she had. Having been in the school for many years, I felt I was in the perfect position to be the intermediary between the faculty and the administration so that together we could fulfill the vision of an outcome-based diploma.

These grandiose plans, however, were abruptly shelved. Within the first month, my journal entries began to fill with the day-to-day stuff that seems to count more than grand plans. Discipline—or at least the attention to quiet halls, orderly lunch rooms, and simple rule adherence—dwindled early in the year. I recount stories of being un-supported in a confrontation with a student, walking in the halls during the last period and thinking there were more students outside classes than inside, going to the office to get help with an unruly student and finding no one there, and feeling that my work on writing and reading was used to show that the school was working hard at establishing outcomes even though no administrator paid much attention to what we were finding or the questions we were asking.

Morale reached such a low point in late October—teachers were talking about the students behaving the way they do in late spring—that I felt we as a faculty should ask for a general meeting with our administrators in order to let them know of our frustrations with the reality of site-based management. We were doing all the work and getting little support or recognition in return. Publicly, the school was being held up as a model for site-based decision making while the faculty felt the school was not a model for anything other than chaos.

At the October Maine Network of School Leaders meeting, I talked to two administrators: one an elementary principal, another a high school assistant principal. They suggested that I use the management system recently developed for bringing issues into the open, the newly established Faculty Council. Despite the efforts of the people on the council, it had not been working well. I had little faith in it and had not thought about it as a solution. But my MNSL colleagues said to focus specifically on the facts (what people saw) and perceptions (how they saw others' actions) to describe what was happening in the school as a platform for trying to solve the problem and deal with the frustrations.

Their advice helped solve the problem—by first making it worse. I recommended to my colleagues on the 11th-grade team that the Faculty Council discuss our concerns about student management at the next meeting. So our team leader brought up the issues, other team leaders chimed in, and the result, according to my team leader, was awful. The administrators felt threatened. They assumed that the entire school was talking about them. My team leader felt that they had taken the remarks much too personally; the conversation had, in fact, degenerated into personal gripes rather than focusing on the major issues. Morale worsened.

When I heard about the meeting, I suggested that as a team we should put our thoughts in writing so that there would be no question about the tone and intent. A letter would clearly indicate our team's concerns, provide a direction for ameliorating the situation, and ask for a response from the administration. So I wrote the letter. The result was several team meetings with the principal where she responded to our view that the school lacked direction. She realized that all of her communication seemed to be out in the larger community and not with the people within the school. I told her that we faculty members needed to see that the administrators did listen to us. We resolved that we needed to bring to the forefront the goals and vision for the school. I felt I was joining her in filling the power vacuum we were all experiencing.

The effects of this "crisis" were very significant for me as a teacher leader. In writing the letter to the principal, I articulated my vision of the school and how I hoped we would get there. By sending it as a team and having it be part of the Faculty Council meeting, my colleagues and I showed our belief in the system *we* had helped to establish. We were part of the solution, too.

Speaking Up Among My Colleagues

My risk taking continued. At the November faculty meeting, teachers from local vocational programs spoke about Tech-Prep. The faculty listened politely to their presentation and dutifully answered their questions, leading us to see how important it was to prepare kids for their vision of the future. Finally, I said that everything these schools were doing was all well and good, but they were acting as if we didn't know what we were doing in preparing kids for future jobs. In addition, what we focus on—the skills of reading, writing, and computing, not to mention researching and problem solving—were pretty vital to skill development in any field. Our school was working toward ensuring that kids could demonstrate those skills in order to go on to school and out into the world and learn more.

After my comments, the faculty meeting ended. Many colleagues approached me and congratulated me for saying what they were thinking and for putting the comments in terms of the performance-based work we had been doing. A "new-to-the-school" teacher said he was thrilled that I spoke up for our curriculum and said that I had put the work of the school in perspective for him.

It was such a simple thing, but it made me realize that I was as guilty of making assumptions and not being explicit about my beliefs as my principal. The value of stating my beliefs carried over to the next meeting of the reading and writing group, the results-based, action-research-into-assessment project that began last year. One teacher had commented at an earlier meeting that his students did not take very seriously the assessment of reading he gave them and we scored. My reply was that we, nevertheless, needed to stand by our new assessment practices. Our work as a committee was totally worthless if we were not incorporating what we were doing as a group into our own classrooms.

In order to support this contention, I gave a test to my students that was very similar to ones we had developed as a group. Then I scored it using the rubric we had developed. I told the reading/writing teachers about it as a demonstration of what I felt we should be doing to move the whole system ahead with regard to our findings. Then I set down in a memo to the members of the group how I thought we could incorporate reading and writing assessment in all of our classes. Many people congratulated me for being so clear; however, one colleague said that I had changed. The letter represented arrogance that he didn't think was characteristic of the real me.

I was both hurt and complimented by this remark. I thought everyone knew that I always looked at things from the teacher's perspective and would never, ever do anything in the least bit uncharacteristic of the humble teacher. At the same time, I was glad to see that I had had an impact. People noticed. My journal reflects some of this ambivalence in this conclusion to an entry in November:

> The more responsibility I have for the direction of the school and for the overall management of a department as it fits into the goals of the school, the less power or authority I feel to actually do anything about it. Maybe I see what a principal sees, how complicated and treacherous is the path.

Nevertheless, I continued to speak out. At a faculty meeting in January, department heads spoke about their work on the diploma project. As the health, math, and social studies lead teachers spoke, I became increasingly concerned that the diploma project was going to degenerate into departmental work that would not be integrated with any other department and thus be just another layer of bureaucracy. I was afraid that we were not making any substantial change in how we do things and what we expect of students.

When I got up to present the proposed reading and writing outcomes, I told people that I would gladly entertain comments from the faculty on the outcomes—in writing. Then I said I thought the whole idea was in danger of going the way of many initiatives—dying in committee or becoming an activity of the school to which people pay lip service, frustrating the people who have worked hard to further the ideals of competencies and outcomes. I said we needed to put some money into the project: We should set up a learning lab for remediation of students who need more help in fulfilling the school's expectations; we should plan for external assessments of student work in some areas for next year; we needed a person or group of people to oversee the work because it could not be done in addition to what we were doing now.

Publicly putting my ideas into words instigated me to further action. I circulated to the Curriculum Council before their next meeting three proposals that directly related to those things I had mentioned at the faculty meeting. The council meeting agenda was to discuss staff and equipment budgets. My proposals dealt with the establishment of a learning lab, a "contracted" position for a person or group to oversee the diploma project, and a change in English offerings to accommodate seniors who have completed expectations as well as those who still need help in meeting the requirements.

At the Curriculum Council meeting, one member said, "Where did this whole learning lab idea come from? All of a sudden everyone is talking about it as if it's going to happen. We're not following the rules we established for how decisions will get made. This group is supposed to make that decision."

I replied, "This is exactly how decisions should get made. When we put proposals in writing, everyone knows what we are talking about and can respond to the ideas. Then we can hammer out a workable plan that is in keeping with our overall goals." When proposals and decisions are not documented, people can say they do not know what has been decided and thus feel no obligation to do anything.

This story illustrates for me some of the major problems of teacher leaders and site-based management. As much as teachers talk about wanting more say in how things are decided, they still expect the principal to guide the process. And when another teacher does take the lead and tries to push things along, as much as others cheer the movement, they are reluctant to allow a fellow teacher to take on the role of leader. I was still so sure of myself, however, that my new-found confidence helped me to rationalize away the resistance of some colleagues. Isn't the "What's fair is equal" view what we are trying to mitigate in our students? So I pushed on.

Dealing With Doubters

In February, I was riding high. The proposals for a learning lab, diploma project coordination, and senior electives provided a clear idea to the Curriculum Council about what the rationale, goals, and budget implications were for all of these plans. Council members, lead teachers of departments in the school, not only agreed that these ideas should be reflected in the budget for next year, but they also implied that future requests, ideas, and suggestions should be in the form of proposals such as this.

The next big triumph of words was when the principal asked me to go with her to a school board meeting to talk about my proposals. She had already put the entire package—along with the outcomes in reading and writing and the rubrics we have been using to assess their fulfillment—in the school board materials for the meeting. This invitation represented a major change. Although we talk a lot about site-based management and, in fact, have created some vehicles for making decisions at the high school, the school board still deals with the principals and holds them totally accountable for whatever goes on in *their* schools. My principal was showing the school board that our school is operating differently. Teachers and teacher committees are making proposals and decisions. The principal recognizes that I am focused about what we as a school need to be doing, so she trusts that I will make it clear to the board.

By March, however, my journal shows some chinks in the plans I was so glibly crowing over. My entry for March 18 reads:

> The major issue I am facing right now is other faculty members complaining that they are left out of the decision-making process. Even though we have a Curriculum Council and a Faculty Council, people still want to be involved in all kinds of nitty-gritty details. Ironically, the most outspoken complainer, CC, attends more meetings than anyone in the school because of all the committees in which she participates. The other day at a Curriculum Council meeting, she brought up the fact that no one had told her that we were going to have two meetings in March. The principal had called an extra meeting because she wanted to have someone from the Coalition of Essential Schools meet with us to talk about how we might avail ourselves of their expertise.
>
> I said that I really felt that we should meet every week because there was so much to do and we should connect more regularly anyway. CC blew up and said that there was no way she could meet any more often because she was already overbooked with PETs, team meetings, and Faculty Council obligations.

Curriculum Council members were astounded by her response, but no one said anything. After we talked about the changes in the English offerings for next year, the science department lead teacher made a proposal for a culminating course for seniors that would combine all core curricula. CC said, "Wait a minute. How can we even think about all of these new things when we don't even have a philosophy of the school?"

My co-teacher and I were flabbergasted. She said, "We do have a philosophy. We worked on it at several different points. Granted it is evolving and there are some inconsistencies, but that's what we're trying to do—develop plans that we check against that philosophy and see if they fit. We have to have the plans as well as the overriding goals."

CC replied, "We have so much going on here. Our plates are too full. How can you say we have a philosophy when we go off in all directions all the time? We never say no to anything."

The rest of us were surprised by this comment. Another lead teacher said, "The problem, CC, is not that we never say no. It's that we never say yes."

That's been the refrain of the week for many of us who are so frustrated by the two steps forward, three steps backward movement of change. What I've been wondering about lately is—

- How can we deal with people like this who want to be part of everything but are naysayers—even when you think they know what's going on and agree with it?
- At what point do you force people to confront their negativity?
- How can you get people to accept what their strengths and weaknesses are with regard to the work that needs to be done? Can they trust others to do their own tasks or parts of the job so they don't have to be part of every single decision?
- How do you move things ahead without letting the concerns/ complaints of a few hold you back too much?

From High to Low

These questions persist even now, and they always will surface where leaders attempt to improve schools. But by April, I was feeling that the Council had generated enough collective momentum that no individual naysayer could stop it. I reflected on the progress I had made as a leader and how far the school had come with my focused, yet collaborative, style. My journal reads like a twelve-step guide to self-esteem:

My role in all of this is to support, encourage, and articulate the plan as we continue to work together on outcomes and accountability in our school. I have confidence in my ability to move forward in other areas to make changes. Not only is there a framework for collaborative work but there is also a clearer overriding goal for me, the participants in my project, and the whole school in working toward outcomes. I am an important cog in the wheel, but there are many other important people in this process. In fact, the greatest lesson for all of us in my project is how much more successful plans and ideas are when they result from a group effort. . . .

The school is responding to outside forces—criticisms of schools, focus on outcome-based education, realities of a chang- ing society—in effective ways because of a culture of collegial- ity and a strong commitment to finding more effective ways of making learning authentic. My thinking, writing, and acting have been important in moving us forward, but even more useful has been the development of other teacher leaders.

In fact, our school is becoming much more what Roland Barth talks about as a community of leaders. We have several fora in which teachers participate in the running of the school— teams, Faculty Council, Curriculum Council. It is a bumpy road, I admit, and we are continually working out the process as we go along, but almost everyone has bought in to the final product even if they disagree about the paths to get there.

Many more faculty members see themselves as teacher leaders who have a vision of the school. They see the impor- tance of the many small parts of the whole. So much work can get done by smaller groups who are trusted to connect to overriding goals. . . . In fact, it is crucial that we are all doing different things, in the areas of planning outcomes and assessments at least, because that is how we will see what works, what we think is important, and how to proceed to make this a whole school enterprise.

We need many types of teacher-leaders or teacher-facilitators. We need risk takers, naysayers, go-slowers, cheerleaders, experimenters, even followers. In other words, we need everyone involved and committed to analyzing and reporting on the results of what he or she is doing. My role is to prod the administration as well as my colleagues to continue to work on goals, expectations, outcomes, accountability and to see them as integral to the work of the entire school.

As I now look back on these lines, I am stunned by my blindness to the realities that lay beneath the surface of the events I was crowing about. In late May, things fell apart. All the wonderful stuff I had been saying and feeling about my school went down the tubes in a single week. True, they went down the tubes for me. Other people, I think—and this is the key to the story—feel that truth and reality won out in the crisis.

Here's the story. The work I had done this year (developing and testing assessments in reading and writing, creating a plan for portfolio assessment, gathering support for a learning lab, and talking to teachers about their work and needs for future implementation of the diploma project) culminated in my writing a state innovative grant that would provide funding for the continuation, documentation, coordination, and communication about the work throughout the school system. The basic idea of the grant was to pay teachers to oversee the work in six areas and to fund a coordinator of the project who would also be a member of the school's Curriculum Council. The grant proposal required support of 75% of the faculty of every school in the system as well as 75% of the school board.

As often happens when grants are written by people who are doing many other things, I talked about the idea with the principal and actually drafted it (along with two other teachers) about 2 weeks before the due date. We got people on the faculty and in the community to look at it and produced an overview and rationale for the faculty teams to vote on a week before the due date. The school board had to approve it simultaneously with the faculty because of their meeting dates. They did. The teachers in the other schools did. The high school faculty did not.

High school team leaders, at the planning team's request, took straw polls in their meetings before the Faculty Council meeting the day before the grant was due. Some people objected on the principle that they didn't like grants; others said that it looked like another bureaucracy; some said that it was too much to think of doing in a year; some said that they had no idea what any of this was about; one person said in his team meeting that he wanted a guarantee that the money would continue to be paid by the school system and not take away from other elements in the budget.

I had been the point person for the grant and was crushed. Incredibly, the principal was unaware that people were resisting supporting the grant. In a phone conversation from our homes, we developed a plan for asking the Faculty Council to come to consensus on how the proposal could be changed to make it palatable to everyone. However, at the Faculty Council meeting, two team leaders could support the grant; two could not. After 2 hours, no one would budge. The two team leaders who did not support the proposal insisted that they had no power to decide for their team what changes in the grant would make it acceptable.

I can make up lots of reasons for why the grant proposal failed to get support. Of course, it is complicated and there probably were many factors at work. But as a teacher who had risked a lot to champion this project, the experience was devastating. It shook my faith in my colleagues, but even more so in myself as a leader. I thought I had such a following, that everything was so clear about what needed to be done, that teachers trusted that I was doing something in their best interests—even if it did mean more work and more meetings.

The basis of my problem was an assumption that people were with me all the way. I believed that my actions and individual connections would produce solid backing from most people and the others would be swept along. I was very hurt and angry about certain people's reluctance to give support to the concept—especially because they were unwilling even to work toward a resolution of their complaints. The principal's lack of critical support, I discovered, was because she herself didn't really understand either the grant or her role in communicating to the faculty why the grant was important. My goals for the school and for myself had been thwarted because others needed more time and coddling to see the where, how, and why of the plan. I felt like a martyr because I had spent all this time and effort for a bunch of ingrates.

So . . . Can Teachers Be Leaders Among Their Equals?

As much as I wanted to quit, sulk, and stop leading after June, I seem to have come out of those feelings without much conscious effort. At the end of the year, everything became so intensified and accelerated that I couldn't dwell on the situation. I had too much to do. And I began seeing some positives in it all. A fair number of people got to voice their concerns about the project and to feel that they had some power over the outcome, albeit a negative one. More importantly, I experienced a big sigh of relief. If this work is to continue, I realized that I can't do it all myself.

The Academy taught me that I need to reflect on experience with some objectivity and distance in order to learn and incorporate those learnings into new behavior. The final events of the school year indicate that I have had ambiguous success. I have had months to mull this over and to wonder if teacher leadership is a viable role. Here are some concluding thoughts.

I'd rather do things myself (I am a Myers-Briggs INFJ). I think that may be one reason why I assumed that things were going along well and that my writing coupled with my actions were enough to bring people along to support me. I don't enjoy processing things and would rather assume people are with me than risk the conflict if they are not. I had always tried to articulate to the principal and superintendent the teacher's perspective, but I didn't tell teachers that. Neither did I make it clear to teachers all the time that I was aligned with them rather than being a quasi-administrator.

I felt, too, that my having been in the school as a teacher and *emerging* leader for so long gave me a strong base of support. But I fluffed over differences of opinion; I neglected to really talk over (or rather really hear) the fear of change and the problems some people had with outcomes work and high standards. Also, as a very definite "N," I have little patience with people who need concrete, sequential steps to get somewhere. And even though I'm a "J," I will change a plan at the drop of a hat if it looks as if some other plan is better. I know that some people on my faculty see me as a circumventer of the rules and established processes or, at least, see themselves as preservers of order and rationality because they are so concerned with rules and rituals.

Confrontation for me is not necessarily arguing and talking; it's often not saying anything at all. I find that I'm much better at stating clearly what I believe in writing. I realize now that can intimidate others. What I perceive as an invitation to respond—preferably in writing—others see as very threatening. Written words have much power. Others may have agreed with me in part, but the weight of the written word overwhelmed them, so they rebelled in any way they could by voting with their feet.

Must I confront, then, my failure as a true collaborator? Have I really been a martinet, all the time thinking I was an equal among equals? Should I recede into the background and let someone else try to do it as well? To all of these questions, I answer, "No." Certainly, I made mistakes. I can take some responsibility for the failure of the grant proposal. I assumed too much about how people were thinking about the diploma project and about my role as the spokesperson for planning and thinking about future implementation. In addition, I am guilty of not taking seriously the power of the site-based management plan we had established at the beginning of the year. I see now that the Faculty Council members who did not support the grant proposal and a few other people feel very satisfied that they did exercise their power in that decision-making body.

But I also contributed to the growth of the faculty as a professional community. Their ownership for curriculum and teaching practices may be stronger and more real as a result of the conflict and tension surrounding the failure of the grant proposal. People had their fears recognized and were able to talk about them openly. The process of decision making was legitimized. More people participated in the discussion about the major issues of the curriculum and what the school is and should be all about.

Finally, my "punched-in-the-stomach" experience has taught me that to be a teacher leader is a double-edged sword. In the society of teachers, it is anathema because it suggests a different status, a fundamental inequality of power. At the same time, teachers really have no choice but to lead because they, above all, control and understand the school's students, curriculum, and learning results.

I learned this year—and certainly it has been said many times before—that schools and faculties must be sure of inclusion, communication, documentation, and protection of the process in our work at changing what we do and how we do it. All teachers must accept leadership roles and model the responsibility we all must bear in the community of learners.

THE MARATHON

---

*A Chapter I Coordinator looks back over her attempts to improve
services and finds that change and leadership require long-distance
stamina.*

Ann Constantine Cheney

When I began my present job as Chapter I Coordinator, I felt well
prepared to deal with change. I had read numerous articles and had
written a lengthy paper. I had observed how difficult even small
changes could be for fellow teachers. Even though I had resisted change
a bit myself, I felt well prepared to breathe new life into Chapter I.
After all, I had observed and learned a lot about change and I had
held various positions of leadership in my school. I knew that change
would require patience and the courage of my convictions and was
sure I had plenty of both.

As with all new administrators, I knew everyone was wondering
what changes I would bring. I could see the worry on the faces of my
assistants, so I reassured my inherited staff that I would not make
enormous changes immediately. For the first year, there were only
building-based changes in the program. I spent this year reading, talking to state Chapter I officials, talking to other Chapter I directors,
talking to teachers, and talking to parents about how children learn to

read. After all that talking, I knew what one change I wanted to make most.

For 17 years our first graders had been instructed in groups of four to six students. They received 30 minutes of instruction per day in addition to their classroom instruction. Usually the group was made up of students from one class, so the Chapter I instruction impacted the life of the teacher for 30-40 minutes each day. Chapter I was strongly respected for its emotional and cognitive support, but instruction was a bit stale. Reading scores had begun to slide, especially in first grade.

I knew I could not change anything or anyone all at once, so I provided weekly workshops to the assistants, giving new philosophies and methods, assuming they would love the new knowledge. Wrong! They had another idea—keep it like it always has been. They resisted the new information:

"What is wrong with the way we do it now?"
"Whole language just doesn't have enough structure for our
   kids."
"This stuff about metacognition just doesn't apply to us. If I
   don't understand what it is, the kids certainly won't."
"I don't understand how I'm going to teach phonics without
   worksheets."

I'm sure there were some positive comments about my presentations but I do not remember these. I felt deflated and wished I had a stronger ego. I felt threatened by the criticism and frustrated that they did not want the theories and methods I was so anxious to share. The race I had entered looked long. I wondered if I had the endurance to run it.

The First Leg: Walk Before You Jog

The change I planned to make seemed simple, timely, necessary, and pleasant. Beginning in the next school year, we would instruct our first graders individually, in a manner similar to Reading Recovery, an early-intervention, highly structured reading program which originated in New Zealand. Backed by a supportive principal and superintendent, I introduced the notion to my staff by inviting a Reading Recovery teacher (and Chapter I state official) to explain the program. I had learned the year before that an outsider might carry more credibility than I did, so I decided to let her describe what we might do. The presentation included slides, information, anecdotes, and support for the change. What did my staff say?

> "That was boring. I could have used some planning time."
> "What's wrong with the way we do it now?"
> "If we work with kids individually, how much could we give them? Ten minutes? It doesn't seem worth it."
> "I don't work with first grade. What does this have to do with me?"
> "That was interesting. What specifically would we do with kids?"
> "How much time would we be able to have the kids? I don't think we could take them all for half an hour each day."

I could see this race lengthening into a marathon, and I could also see that the run would be mostly uphill. To get the change off to a good start during the implementation year, I made an executive decision. First graders would receive 1 day of individual instruction each week. The other days would remain the same as they always were. Small change first; walk before you jog. We didn't discuss this decision much. I had received feedback from my staff that they wanted more decisions, less talk. What they really wanted were more decisions they agreed with!

My district acquired a new superintendent who asked a lot of questions about my program and my plans for the future. She had notions about Chapter I that did not match mine; for example, she was very interested in implementing more inclusion. But she was also willing to support my plans about individual instruction for first graders with two additional part-time teachers.

This year's change happened reasonably smoothly. Feedback about 1 day of individual instruction was positive. My assistants rather liked having students alone. Teachers tolerated the change in their schedule, because it only involved 1 day each week. Students liked it best of all. Not only did they enjoy the time with their Chapter I teachers, but they also seemed to benefit academically in the one-to-one situation.

I was in the race for the long haul, but the run was easier because I was not alone. We were working together in this change process; administrators, assistants, parents, students, and I were very hopeful. I even dared to think I might have talent for this leadership business. I was instituting change faster than I had expected and it was quality change. What I couldn't see was that this small change was necessary and relatively easy, but it was only a leisurely jog.

Step Up the Pace . . . and Believe in Yourself

I thought we were ready for the big change—individual instruction for the entire first grade. We visited a variety of schools that were offering individual instruction. We continued to talk about the change; I admitted that I was learning along with the rest. My plan was to structure the best plan for reading instruction as we tried it out. I did not insist on any one particular method at this point, but our visits and the focus of our meetings led in the direction of the Reading Recovery model. I am very comfortable trying out new methods as I go, and I felt increasing confidence in my staff. I knew they would do a fine job with whatever methods they were using.

As it turned out, I should have told my staff about my confidence in them. I should have asked them about their confidence in trying out new methods. Perhaps they would have been more comfortable during this uncertain phase. Classroom teachers were now strongly impacted by the change. Students were being pulled from classrooms all throughout the day. Teachers could not easily keep track of which student missed which lesson. Some Chapter I teachers were happy; most were not:

> "My students are way ahead. I don't have to hold them back now. They can go ahead more than when they were held back by the slower members of the group."
> "I don't like it at all. I can't use my units with only one child and I have to read the same story six or seven times."

"It is repetitious to do the same thing over and over. Some of
    the kids are bored, too."
"I don't think this program is working. Could we go back to
    groups?"

I had hit the wall. I wanted to give up. Let instruction go back to
the old way. Maybe I was wrong to try to facilitate this change.

Luckily, the parents were delighted with our change. Specifically,
they cited increases in students' self-confidence as a result of our individual instruction. Students were happy and learning to read. Classroom teachers reported good progress by the students. This was
enough to keep me going. Our test scores did not match the positive
effects we saw in the students, but I felt supported by my superintendent and principal, as well as by parents and students. The literature
on individual instruction and especially Reading Recovery was reporting strong success, so I felt it was only a matter of time before
everyone saw how things were improving. I was getting my second
wind.

Surviving a Stiff Headwind

We opened a new elementary school the next fall, splitting students and staff into two buildings. Decisions about which staff and
students would be at each school were painful. Staff was divided and
a profound sense of loss was present. It was hardly the time for program changes; there was a lot of adjustment to the changes already
brought on by the split. A significant opportunity for yet another
change arrived with the new principal who took over the leadership
of the older school. But she did not believe in any Chapter I services
for first graders! She contended that first graders should get a year of
uninterrupted classroom instruction, then be remediated in Grade 2 if
they had not made sufficient reading progress.

My philosophy of earliest-possible intervention was in direct op-
position to hers, and we had some challenging conversations. I saw
this as a hurdle and was determined to clear it. I explained how Reading Recovery uses the same format each day. Such repetition gives
readers confidence and success. Students read real books that have

been selected for their reading level. Nonreaders or beginning readers may read books that have picture clues and only one word on a page. They learn phonics in context; there are no worksheets as such, but it is a heavily phonetic program. Above all, the students are reading for meaning.

I held the advantage when I set out to convince this principal of the merits of my instructional plan. My years of classroom reading instruction gave me some influence with the staffs in both schools. I have the reputation of being thorough, knowledgeable about theory, and conservative when it comes to change. Teachers trust me because they know I do not change easily; in spite of some resistance from the Chapter I teachers, the teachers as a whole were behind me.

I invited my principal to watch instruction in classrooms. I used the needs assessment surveys from first-grade teachers and their evaluations of the first-grade program the previous year; these surveys reported the students' skill growth and their increased self-esteem. Lastly, I used the research that was suggesting that early intervention and individual instruction is the most effective way to give language remediation. When the year was over, she said, "I've changed my mind; you've convinced me." I had survived a stiff headwind and could now regain my pace.

My Staff Provides a Tailwind

We were now accommodating classroom teachers better by taking four or five students from a classroom at a time. There was strong support from both principals and the superintendent. Parents reported that they were very pleased with the program. The students were thriving. The number of students referred to our program for reading increased by more than 50%. My confidence jogged along at a comfortable pace.

I had the good fortune to acquire a Reading Recovery teacher who gave us many useful strategies to make the program even better. I began to think the finish line was in sight. I felt great satisfaction at this point, having believed in this change and stuck by my beliefs even when challenged. One Chapter I teacher commented, "You went through a lot to get us all to believe in this change. I know it was hard at times, but I admire you for sticking to it." High praise indeed.

This change to individual instruction with an emphasis on Reading Recovery may appear to be a small change. However, it was a major change for the teachers in our Chapter I program. I certainly did not think it would take more than 5 years to complete. But I am convinced that the change happened so slowly because there was really nothing wrong with the old instruction; children were learning to read. We just wanted our instruction and student learning to be that much better. There had been little, if any, change in reading instruction for years though. No one had practiced the skills needed to make it happen. Change is real work and it is hard. We changed slowly, but as we did it, we were open to other views and this made us thorough and careful. Ultimately, this participation will make the change last.

Just when I thought I had experienced all I could, I learned that my Chapter I assistants wanted to make further changes in the program. They felt that some students might need a different approach or a variety of approaches:

"Not all our students need this level of intervention."
"Some of the students have less severe needs. We need to modify the approach for them."
"A few students have identifiable learning disabilities by the middle of the first grade. We need to deal with these students."
"What about those students who just don't learn with Reading Recovery? What about them?"

You might think that these recommendations by my assistants would have made me happy; they were keeping their minds open to new ideas and developments I had not anticipated at the beginning of the project. They were being objective and thorough. Instead, I reacted by being defensive about having my ideas challenged. I had held onto the principle of individual instruction through Reading Recovery for so long, had fought so hard for its acceptance, that it had become a marathon to win at any cost. When they suggested that we might look at different approaches to our instruction, I saw this as yet another challenge and dismissed the idea.

But they kept trying. They showed me the work of children who were having success in the classroom with methods not akin to Reading Recovery. They reminded me that Reading Recovery is intended for the very poorest readers. They pointed out that we have readers who are only 6 months below the norm for first grade; we should expect their needs to be considerably different from the needs of the poorest readers. I also reviewed the research and found their ideas supported. Finally, I said, "I've changed my mind. You've convinced me."

I was surprised at my stubbornness. It blinded me to some terrific new ideas. These observations and learnings make sound educational sense. Students learn in so many different ways; no one way or method is right for all. The staff had become a tailwind to propel me and, most importantly, our students to new finish lines!

I learned a lot from reflecting about the events in this marathon. I learned that change is threatening. It implies that the "old way" was less than perfect. Change is also uncomfortable and uncertain. I learned to have a long supply of patience with others who are accepting change. I learned that this patience is not enough, nor is a great educational plan. What is also needed is time for all the runners to really become part of the race, to own the change and want to finish the process.

Change is more effective when the obstacles are anticipated, but this is usually not the case, and if the change is a worthy one, the unexpected obstacles can be overcome. Sound educational ideas are slowly woven into school life; quick change does not last.

I learned that change requires strong leaders with durable convictions. I also learned that those leaders need to examine their own beliefs, abilities, and willingness to embrace change along the way. It was easier for me to help others with change than it was to reflect on what changes I needed to make myself. I am still struggling with this marathon, but I am less concerned with winning. The end is less important to me than it was before. After all, in change there is no finish line.

ALONE AT SEA:
Maneuvering Through a
School's Culture

A high school teacher describes how isolation discouraged her attempts to lead and how she persevered to influence her school for the benefit of students.

Martha G. Corkery

For the greater part of my 16 years as a secondary school teacher, I have been at sea without benefit of charts, without the food or equipment necessary for survival, and without companionship. In spite of pouring my heart and soul into my work with students and being a tireless advocate for children, I have had to struggle to survive and earn a place as a legitimate educator and as a leader of school improvement. Ironically, I have always presented myself as the epitome of strength: I have been deeply involved in initiatives, held numerous leadership positions, and have a reputation as a risk taker. I have been sustained and motivated by doing my very best for my students.

But as I have challenged the status quo, I have received little acknowledgment, and I have felt that my talents have been poorly utilized in my school. I have had few opportunities for personally meaningful professional development, and rare occasions for ongoing collaboration with colleagues. I have found little support and encouragement, and the eyebrows I have raised have only reconfigured themselves to permanent frowns when I have raised difficult questions.

With few exceptions, my efforts to improve my school led to an isolated existence for me, one in which I felt typecast as a rabble-rouser. It has left me feeling as though I have been kicked in the teeth. Ironically, this writing piece will cause me yet again to break the taboo of silence. I realize I am only one voice but my experiences are real and are valid to me. When this piece is read, I anticipate the frowns will deepen and spread to more faces. My reason for writing about my experiences is not to cast blame or vent anger, but to make sense of my experience by sharing it with others. I can only hope that the resulting frowns will not be aimed at my boldness in saying what I have to say, but will spring from a recognition of the conditions under which some of us work in schools.

Perhaps my story is unique to me. But I wonder if the codes of silence and isolation in schools are the true culprits in making educators believe their professional experiences are unique to them. Is this more than the untold story of just one teacher?

Rudderless in Rough Waters

I marvel at my longevity in this profession. From the time I first began working with my students, I knew intuitively that something was wrong. School was not working for these students and it certainly was not working for me. My heart sank when I saw how effortlessly my veteran colleagues glided through the tribulations of a school day, knowing full well what they hoped to accomplish. I felt inadequate and wondered how long it would take until I figured out the "secret." I tried to determine what tack I might take in finding the answer to my uncertainty as a professional, and without anyone telling me, I somehow understood that task was mine alone.

After wallowing in my feelings of ineptness, I decided to seek companionship in the search. Although I knew you didn't talk about what you didn't know as a teacher, I wouldn't be able to complete this journey successfully without camaraderie. In an effort to access their expertise, I decided I would ask my department colleagues for this assistance.

I recall at one of our department meetings announcing that the materials I used were not working. I asked for suggestions and ideas about what to do for these "tough" students. The resulting silence and knowing side glances made me squirm. I wished I could stuff my words back into my mouth. Much later in my career, I realized I had violated the code that served as an underpinning for the design of secondary schools: ISOLATION + INDEPENDENCE = COMPETENCE. At the time I had no idea how significantly that particular incident would influence the remainder of my stay in that building. I had no idea, either, how it would mark me as incompetent simply because I had asked for help. My desired outcome was to gain from the expertise and knowledge of my colleagues but instead, I soon discovered, they began to question my ability to teach.

Several days after I had posed my question to the department, Melvyn, a fellow department member and later department chair, offered me some advice: "You know, Martha, raising a family is a noble profession and there would certainly be nothing wrong with that. You might find that to be most rewarding to you."

Realize, of course, I had no plans to marry nor did I express any desire to have a family. In addition, I was hearing Melvyn use the same line with students as he advised them to make career decisions and select colleges. I said nothing and shared this with no one as I felt at the time there was no one I could trust. I also realized if I aligned myself with the "wrong" people, my reputation might incur further damage. I floated along without any direction at all.

I recall too how my principal, Darryl, teased me relentlessly in front of my colleagues. He would say things like, "Martha, I think I'll give you a pink slip at the end of the year. You really shouldn't have your contract renewed, now should you?" Instead of offering me support or advice as I worked with some of the most difficult students in the school, he was making me doubt myself even more. My only choice was to do what every good teacher was doing in those days—grin and bear it—knowing full well things were not working. Whenever these kinds of comments were made, my insecurities and understanding of the problems in my classroom were highlighted. I didn't, however, have what I needed to address the problems and had no visible channels for accessing that which I needed.

I worked very hard and became frustrated at the benefits my hard work failed to reap for my students. In spite of a number of discussions with Darryl about my needs, he included this sentence in my evaluation: "Martha has a very negative attitude." I asked him to remove the comment and indicated that I was frustrated and told him why. Darryl never did much to help me out beyond removing that sentence from my evaluation. Needless to say, I had no idea whether or not I could cut it as a teacher.

In retrospect, I believe most of my colleagues' initial responses to me were quite unintentional and very much a part of the norms governing this school. Unfortunately, in later encounters, I became a victim of that norm and was placed in a box that perhaps few of my associates would ever recognize because they were so busy and the culture was so ingrained in us. We seldom stepped back to consider what was happening to us or to our colleagues. Over the years, I felt pain and anger as I was told why I couldn't have certain teaching assignments and why I was not the "right person" to perform certain leadership tasks. How could I have gone from being a bright, self-assured high school and college leader and a highly successful student teacher to being so uncomfortable, insecure, and unappreciated? I continued drifting, realizing my course may not be as clear as I had once thought, still finding no colleague with whom I might plot a course.

A Breeze Brings Hope, Then Hopelessness

"Martha, you are much too sensitive. If you are going to stay in education and work with administrators and people like us, you have to grow a thicker skin. You have to roll with the punches," said Eric, another administrator, most authoritatively. I wondered what he meant by "people like us" and if that was something I should aspire to. For some reason, I felt a wind building behind me.

I lifted the mainsail high on the mast, expecting to head in a wonderful new direction. I "thickened my skin" and took the risk of running for the Staff Development Committee; in fact, I did so on several occasions. Each time the election was held in the morning and the victorious teachers were to attend the Staff Development Committee that afternoon. Each time, I planned to be available in case I was successful. I never attended one of those afternoon staff development meetings. Now, I needed that thick skin! Once again, I faced the dead calm, alone.

I began to feel oddly like the tough kids I had in my classes. In fact, my situation and that of my students were frighteningly parallel. They were being told what they had to learn without explanation and were expected to follow blindly. As a teacher, I was to behave in a certain manner and obey certain norms, without knowing why. Oblivious to exactly what was happening to me, I began to act on my self-doubt by actively pursuing a job with the post office. I stopped short of taking the postal exam. In spite of my frustration and self-doubt, something drew me back to teaching.

Then, out of the blue, one of my colleagues extended a hand to me. A fellow teacher, Sean, invited me to become part of a study skills team that was to share successful study skills strategies with other teachers. Sean had recognized in me some of the same feelings he was experiencing as a change agent. We soon realized how "unready" teachers were for anyone to share with them. They may like the ideas, but there was a suspicion whenever one teacher demonstrated expertise or knowledge about something—the antithesis of what's necessary in a learning environment. The sail filled with wind as we raced ahead, together. Then, our initial task complete, our group disbanded. A short time later, I was stunned to learn that Sean had decided to leave teaching to sell real estate. My sole comrade was gone. The wind died. Once more I was on my own, adrift.

When Sean left, college-track teaching positions opened up. I requested assignment to some of his college sophomore groups. When I asked about the position, Melvyn responded, "We're looking for someone with an American history background." Had I still not paid my dues or had all of this been a result of that strained moment when I asked for assistance my first year in the school? I felt myself accepting the fact that others saw something lacking in me. Perhaps I deluded myself into thinking I was someone I was not.

During the same time period, I asked the teachers' association president, Al, if I could be a negotiator or a building representative. Al told me, "We don't need anyone now, but if you'd like you can hand out these pledge sheets on Friday." I never saw the forms on Friday. In fact, I was not invited to do anything for years.

Then our building administrator handpicked a group of faculty members to attend a meeting about school restructuring. Despite the fact that I had been stretching and contorting the system for my students for years, I had not been included on the list. I heard about the meeting over lunch and my little boat ran aground. My level of rejection rose to an all-time high and I felt my desire to continue as a teacher waning and my enthusiasm as dry as the ground beneath my boat. I needed something beyond the classroom, although I may have been unable to articulate that at the time. I also had this need to give more so that I could "get more." My spirit had reached its breaking point.

Changing Course

Fortunately, before his departure, Sean had planted a life-saving seed. One day he told me, "Martha, you should enroll in the literacy program at the university. It has made me a much better teacher and opened my eyes to so many things about teaching." I decided I would apply to graduate school. By this time I had been employed with the school district for 7 years and decided I should apply for a sabbatical. After another long struggle with colleagues over this much needed professional development opportunity, I was granted a sabbatical leave.

Once in graduate school and working on my Master's degree, some amazing things happened to me. They were amazing because they were so contrary to my experiences as a teacher. I was hired to be a full-time graduate assistant for two literacy professors. I assisted them in gathering research for their book, and they asked me to develop a teachers' manual to accompany their text. When I would talk about the work I did with students, my mentors and fellow graduate students would express their enthusiasm for my talents as a teacher. On several occasions, Peter, one of the professors with whom I worked, asked me to present in his undergraduate and graduate courses. I remember him introducing me to those groups of educators in the following manner: "I'd like you to meet Martha Corkery. Martha is a master teacher who teaches at Leihigh Central School. She is part of our program this year, and we hope to learn from her while she's with us." While studying at the university, I conducted workshops for school districts, acted as a consultant, and was asked to teach an undergraduate reading course. The result: My self-doubt blossomed into self-confidence. I felt rejuvenated professional curiosity. My vessel had never glided as quickly and effortlessly over the water as it did at this point in my career. I was collecting the nourishment and equipment I needed to make my voyage more meaningful.

As the academic year drew to a close, I began to worry about how I could maintain this excitement and enthusiasm for my work back at school. The negativity of colleagues and culture threatened to overwhelm me. So I began to plan my escape. Madge, my other literacy mentor, had told me she'd love to have me continue working with the interns in their teacher education program. Funds were questionable, but she suggested I speak directly to the dean. In the name of self-preservation, I arranged a meeting with my superintendent and the dean of the College of Education. We talked about my future. At that point, I would have made a deal with the devil himself NOT to go back to Leihigh Central School. It certainly wasn't the students or how I could use all my new knowledge that concerned me—it was how I felt when I was there. I didn't want to be set adrift again.

At any rate, we had a wonderful discussion, quite wonderful in that these two administrators took the time to discuss my situation and assist me in determining my next tack. The dean indicated she would love to keep me at the university, but there wasn't anything available due to budgetary restrictions. The superintendent indicated that my failure to return would create problems for other teachers who sought sabbatical leaves. I considered how vital the sabbatical leave had been for me and promptly decided that I would not jeopardize my colleagues' opportunities for such an experience. The logic and sincerity of these two women helped me to make an intelligent decision, but intuitively I knew things would change for me for only a short period of time.

Will the New Chart Work in Old Waters?

In light of my decision, the issue of being alone at sea loomed ahead for me. But now my school looked different to me. My time on the outside had helped me understand why I had felt so left out. There was a power structure in the school with some teacher empowerment; unfortunately only a few teachers were empowered. I had not been one of the empowered ones, but now I realized that neither were *most* of my colleagues. What a discovery that was for me! Having observed the functioning of the school from afar had broadened my perspective and heightened my awareness of the culture of our school and the need for that climate to change. I also realized that if I wished to positively impact our school's culture, I had to be in a position that would allow me to do so.

Six years after my first unsuccessful attempts to influence the school as a whole, I ran for staff development again and won the election. Even though I had been unopposed, I realized I had to take advantage of this new opportunity.

I frequently spoke out at staff meetings and my new role began to take shape. I would ask questions—questions no one else asked. When we began changing the school schedule, I asked, "Why are we doing this?" When a committee I was chairing had developed an advisory program curriculum for every teacher to implement with every student in the school and it appeared not to work, I asked, "Is this really educationally sound? Isn't this like all being on the same page on the same day? Is this really good teaching?" I didn't let the code of silence inhibit me. I had played the game for years and it didn't work. I became a squeaky wheel. I had discovered my voice and selected a course.

After a time, I decided that I might be able to help change the structures that weren't working by assuming a more significant leadership role in the school change process. When I was eventually voted into one of two school restructuring coordinator positions, unopposed, a colleague anonymously wrote on an evaluation sheet, "The process we used to elect the coordinator was silly and we even ended up with the wrong person getting elected." My fellow staff development folks called attention to the note but indicated I shouldn't take it personally. How else could I take it? I wondered! I decided to stay on course and not look back.

During that same year, I observed the teachers' association in constant battle with the superintendent. She was obviously supportive of teachers yet the association continued to treat her in an adversarial manner. I didn't believe that sort of relationship was necessary. I was interested in shifting the association into a more collaborative role, and I believed that the superintendent and I could do a great deal together for the school district. I had toyed with taking a leadership role in the association before because the possibility of running an organization and advocating for teachers appealed to me. I knew my ability to raise questions and my passion for children and public education would fit nicely into this role. I quietly considered this agenda as the wind continued to fill my sails.

So I deep-sixed my self-doubt and ran for association president! I was elected in a contested race. I now found myself wearing *two* hats: as restructuring leader and association president. Oddly enough, association leadership provided me with smoother sailing and greater opportunities for leadership autonomy than did the school leadership position.

As a restructuring coordinator, I communicated with all teachers, regardless of which camp they might be in. I tried very hard to make the staff development committee cognizant of the absolute necessity for teacher buy-in and respect for where people were developmentally. My message was not heard and I felt as though I was being swallowed up by the bureaucracy of school leadership.

The association presidency offered me a better chance to establish a form of leadership that worked for me. When some of my more innovative colleagues urged me to edge out my predecessor and those who had formerly held positions of power in the association, I instead worked harder to involve these folks. I had my fill of exclusion! As a result, our association belongs to everyone and I am not viewed as an extreme liberal. The most exciting part of my leadership accomplishments is that my successes are not mine alone. I know that without having shared those successes with others, they would have been pointless activities.

Over the summer, I met with the new superintendent. Although I would have enjoyed working with our former superintendent, part of my motivation for seeking the presidency had been the new superintendent. I saw an opportunity for breaking the adversarial tradition. At our meeting I explained that there was a certain degree of disharmony among our 10 buildings. I indicated that this disharmony impacted the association as well. I ventured even further to suggest that we could work together to create a sense of harmony in the district, or we could do it separately. I announced my choice of collaboration but left the final decision to him. He said he would try working together.

I worked to develop a number of new vehicles for facilitating change within the local association. The constitution and bylaws were rewritten by myself and a colleague who was particularly adept with such documents. We redesigned the documents so that power typically possessed by the president was shared and so that the representatives from each building would make the major association decisions. Their willingness to become involved was rewarded with responsibility, a shared responsibility. The Executive Committee had come to understand, without labeling it as such, shared decision making.

We worked to establish a new standing committee, the innovations committee. This committee, designed to bring together forward thinking teachers from all six schools to discuss school improvement, served as a foundation for K-12 that is central to the current plan for change in the district. This pulled in teachers who had been disenchanted with the association and expanded the role and structure of the association as well.

The Journey Continues

During my tenure as association president, I began to recognize in myself a need to change every organization with which I became associated. I wondered why I just couldn't be quiet and go along with the crowd. The more we saw links between the association's work and the district's restructuring needs, the more I saw leadership as a single responsibility. When I think about that now, I wonder if my restlessness was caused by my need to step into a leadership vacuum.

I am most miserable when there is nothing for me to change or to challenge. Unbeknownst to me, the association offered endless possibilities along these lines. I have since recognized some of those challenges: most prominent among them, redefining processes and procedures. These are the same issues every organization tackles as it goes through the change process. I internalized much about the change process and how to get people with varying philosophies on board. It was in my association leadership role that I discovered solutions to the cultural issues that I had faced as a teacher and that I had unsuccessfully impacted as a restructuring coordinator.

In spite of many obstacles, I have persevered in this profession for 16 years and have emerged as an educational leader. I have discovered how to survive at sea without benefit of charts, without the food or equipment necessary for survival in such a circumstance, and without substantial companionship. With that knowledge under my belt, I can surely sustain myself and assist my colleagues on their voyages. As a leader, I have learned to make the charts and to catch the breezes to move us forward. And I have vowed that my colleagues will encounter at least one companion who will not allow them to be alone at sea.

FROM RUNNING RAPIDS TO RUNNING A SCHOOL

An elementary teaching principal learns about himself as a school leader from his canoe treks in the Quebec wilderness.

Donald Buckingham

As we filtered our Scotch through the mosquitoes hovering around our mouths, Tulp mentioned that the article that attracted us to the Pretty River talked about some of the hardships faced—long carries, insects of incredible hardiness, poor weather. But James Raffan, the author, also mentioned in the same line, the incredible beauty with which he was rewarded at every turn. Rapids and falls of great power and splendor were worth carrying around. Sunsets and moonrises were magnificent in spite of the constant swatting. The sight of caribou emerging from the fog rewarded our efforts. Neither Tulp nor I considered these hardships, but the price of admission. (Authors's note: All extracts are summaries from my personal journals unless otherwise noted.)

For the past 20 years, I have been enthralled by canoe tripping. It is one of the primary reasons I live in Maine. It is my escape and my teacher. In many ways my ambitions in canoeing parallel my professional ambitions. I envision, propose, recruit, plan, and execute canoe trips the same way I attack challenges at school. The difference is that a canoe trip is a finite, concrete experience with little or no stress for me because of the confidence and self-reliance that I have achieved over the years. I have not yet reached that point as a principal.

On a canoe trip, competence ensures comfort and survival and incompetence can be disastrous. The woods or bush can be the most pleasant or unforgiving of places in the world, depending on one's level of competence. Additionally, there is an element of style, panache, that comes with doing something well that has always been attractive to me. In canoeing I have to decide constantly about which stretches of river I am capable of running and which I must carry around. The exhilaration of running a rapid well and the consequences of a wrong decision are clear to the cognoscente and invisible to the neophyte. Oftentimes, neophytes survive a few bad decisions, but the cumulative impact of poor decision making can be deadly. Occasionally, a few beginners don't get the chance to make other mistakes.

Serving as a principal is at once less finite and less forgiving than canoe tripping. This narrative traces some of my recent learning as a school leader. As with any good trek, it follows a familiar structure:

- Motivation
- Planning
- Doing it
- Return and reflection

Motivation

When the formal process of application to the Maine Academy for School Leaders began in December of 1991, I was in the advanced planning stages of a trip to the Ungava Peninsula of Quebec that would mark my most ambitious canoeing project to date and served in my mind as the point where I was going to be joining the "big boys" of Canadian wilderness canoeing. I needed to get away and wanted to test my skills against a previously unvisited area. Several years earlier I had been given a copy of a National Geographic book that discussed the first descent of an isolated river in northern Quebec. The pictures and article totally blew me away, and it struck me as a destination to aspire to, but I had other irons in the fire—a trip to Labrador and an ambitious 10-day trip in northern Maine with some 16-year-olds, so to the back of my mind it went. Still, the pictures haunted me and I wondered what it would be like to go and see for myself. What about the weather, bugs, isolation? Could I handle the white water and extensive carries? Could I figure the logistics? The reality was, once I'd seen the article, the gauntlet had been thrown down.

After 8 years as a teaching principal and part way through my 3rd year at Sedgwick Elementary School, I was looking for a way to broaden my experiences in leadership and attempting to make the most of any opportunity to talk shop with my colleagues. I was comfortable and happy in my role and school, and was receiving recognition for my efforts in Sedgwick, yet I had a certain uneasiness about where I was going personally and professionally. I was especially worried about where my past professional experiences, which were not all successful, fit with my current ones and what that was telling me about myself as a leader and a person. I was in the process of achieving a large number of major professional and personal goals and, without necessarily being conscious of it, searching for a greater depth of understanding about myself and a better clarification of my professional vision. In many ways, I was trying to determine why, despite achieving my goals, I was still feeling that it was rather undeserved and fortuitous. I was unsure of my place relative to other administrators and teachers.

At the same time, other strands of my life were reaching critical points. My kids were reaching a level of maturity where it was fun to be with them. My absentee parenting was not popular with my wife, a teacher also. I was struggling and unhappy with the imbalance in my roles as father, husband, human, teacher, and principal. The professional recognition I received was offset by pestering personal questions. Could I sustain my success? Could I reconcile the mistakes I had made in the past with what I had learned from them? Could I balance my many roles and be happy? Did I want to stay in educational administration? Could I hold my own with established administrators and "play with the big boys"?

Planning

The make-or-break phase of any canoe trip is in the planning. You can have a wonderful time or kill yourself in the wilds at home in January. In late 1990 I started the process of research- ing the area that I was hoping to visit. I'll call it Pretty River. Since it has been rarely visited, there were very few written resources available and I began trying to find paddlers who had visited the general area, finally striking up a correspon- dence with the author of the article I had read in National Geo- graphic and a paddler who had been into that neck of the woods a couple of years before. I sent off to Ottawa for maps and pored over them on winter afternoons. I contacted charter pilots and estimated costs and types of planes.

I successfully convinced my friend John Tulp, my first choice as partner, that it couldn't possibly be as bad as it looked in the article. I saved money for the exorbitant charter flights. By summer 1991, John and I were ready to sit down and talk turkey. In short order, he became my reality check and my care- fully made plans, dreams really, were out the window as be- ing unrealistic. Back to research and the drawing board with more poring and planning over maps. By spring 1992, we had a plan in place, flight quotes and dates lined up, and we were ready.

As an administrator, I had rarely faced a formal evaluation pro- cess that actually measured my leadership potential. Even when I didn't think I was doing a good job, my superintendents wrote great things about me. It was always amazing to me that they could see so far from their offices. My goals were up to me, and my sense was that my continued employment was based on how I was viewed in my position by the townspeople with the loudest voices.

Planning to improve my leadership took a lot longer than I thought. First, I had to figure out who I was as a leader, what the features of my leadership "maps" were. Self-examination through instruments like the Myers-Briggs introduced me to myself as a school leader. It gave me a language in which to articulate some aspects of myself. My Academy colleagues' openness and honesty showed me other aspects of myself and that other leaders faced the same intense self-doubt that I was trying to resolve.

My success as a principal led me to think that I knew who I was and where I was going, but I didn't know a lot of the particulars, so I didn't really have a clue about what changes were going to be essential to improving my leadership. Without a clear understanding of how I worked as a leader, I could not see how changing myself really worked. The crucial elements missing were the voices of my fellow travelers, the staff, students, and parents of my school. I failed to take into account the reality that others impact me. If my plan was to be less autocratic, then I should have started by admitting that others were going to be instrumental in the changes that I would need to make. At most, I gave them lip service.

> As Tulp and I reviewed the maps on that rainy night in August of 1991, it became clear to me that all my work in planning routes and gathering information was coming to the wrong end. My plan was fraught with cabin fever dreams. As we drank a nice wine in the bare light bulb ambiance of Lu's house, John systematically and politely picked apart my plan. Driving home I didn't need a reminder that the problem wasn't my efforts, or necessarily the plans, which were "doable," but with my failure to remember that someone else was coming along.

My problems with leadership were the result of not understanding the roles that others play in the management and leadership of our schools. I didn't see that schools are really collectives that embody the ideas, sweat, and love of many. Students, parents, teachers, and support staff all contribute to the blend of leadership that I hope to be able to articulate and facilitate.

Doing It

The night before we left to head off to Quebec, Tulp came over with steaks and wine and we reviewed the lists and went over the plans one more time. Rising at 4 a.m., we were on the road at 4:30 and got only 30 miles to Bucksport before we made our first wrong turn. We were just outside of Montreal when we remembered that John's boots were still in his car at my house. We arrived in Radisson at noon the following day after 24 hours of driving and a brief nap and argued with the flight operations manager about the size of the plane we needed. We were off the lake at 1:00 and landed at Pretty Lake on a lovely sunny afternoon at 3:30. Our pilot, Stéfan, was off 15 minutes later and there we were, 250 miles from nowhere, hoping that John's boots were all that we had forgotten. Under my navigation, we paddled confidently off down a long arm of the lake I had been examining on the map for the last 2 years. We found it to be a dead end and not the long arm at all. I have to admit my first reaction to this error was "Uh-oh, what am I doing here!" It took me a while to orient the map in my mind to the reality of being there.

I spent a hot couple of hours in front of a hostile audience a while back. I guess maybe it isn't quite true to say that the people were hostile, although in many ways it would have been easier to write off the incident had they really been boiling the tar and fluffing the feathers. Part of our guidance curriculum was being assailed by a group of parents who were inflamed by some literature from a religious right newspaper. My reaction to these types of problems in the past has been sort of "screw you—this isn't a religious issue and it's my call to make."

But this time around, I had committed myself to questioning my map and to listening to what others were saying beneath the rhetoric of the "cause" that they were fighting for. I tried to see this audience's concerns as the legitimate concerns of parents about who controls their kids and how they are controlled. I took advantage of several discussions I subsequently had with parents, a local minister, and trusted advisors to try to get beyond the hyperbole that so often accompanies such conflicts and gain an understanding of the human and family issues that started the arguments and "stand taking" that makes real resolution of conflicts so difficult. As the principal in the small town where I live and the parent of children in my own school, I tried now to see the parents' concerns from their own side of things. They are, after all, my neighbors, parents of my children's playmates, and because of this familiarity there are friendships and understandings at stake as well as school issues. Because I am "of the community," it was imperative for me to take the time to listen and act on the basis of what I heard and saw for myself, rather than give a "knee-jerk liberal" response that compelled me to simply write off the complaints as ridiculous.

In talking with, rather than at, parents, I saw their concerns about our guidance program as more than a political and cultural straw man to knock down. I had the chance to reflect on who these parents are and their roles in the community. We continually decry the abysmal levels of parental involvement in children's lives and push for more and more. These parents were concerned about more than *their* involvement with their children. They were worried that the *school* was too involved with them. Their fear, religious convictions aside, was that the school, representing some sort of institutional morality, would overwhelm the lessons they were trying to teach at home. They were doing exactly the things that we have been screaming at parents to do for years.

Almost all parents are primarily concerned with the well-being of their kids and really want to do well by them. It may be difficult for us to see this because in our jobs the focus of our attention is too often the cases of abuse we must report or the parent irrationally screaming at us. Teachers and parents sometimes live in mutually exclusive worlds. Teachers and parents do not always agree on the intersection of school and home values. In areas of school curriculum where the intersection is the perceived "control" of a child's actual thoughts and identity, the conflict becomes greatest among those parents who see their ability to guide their own kids as of paramount importance. In my town, these have turned out to be very thoughtful people able to express their fears and problems with the school in an intelligible way.

As I have waded into the white water of the interpersonal element of my community, I see some of the more subtle aspects of the situation more clearly. In looking and listening harder to parents, I've learned to see beyond the banners that we fly as school administrators and teachers. I have learned to understand my schooling map in terms of the realities I encounter. I see that religion and guidance are not the real issue. The issue is in large part the nature of the parent-child-school relationship.

We all—school and parents—must be linked by a common bond that I choose to call values. Our common bond is our common map for working together for our children. To forge that bond, we each must adjust our beliefs to the other's. As long as we persist in thinking our own map is the only map, we are destined to squander any credibility we have worked so hard to build. We end up at the head of a dead-end bay, just as Tulp and I had.

So, I must listen, listen, listen to parents without bringing my own views into play until I have carefully considered what the people are saying to me and before judging if it will fit and how it will fit within established school philosophy and practice. Too often in the past, I have failed to consider the sources of such complaints seriously and failed to see the nature of the issue. Only by examining and articulating the problem can we arrive at a solution. That solution may not always be a resolution, but at least we have a common map on which the conversational journey can begin.

> My Duluth pack weighed in at about 110 pounds. After the first carry, I paused to consider what I could have possibly left behind. Unfortunately, it's not until the end of the trip that you can make a determination about what you could have left behind or should have brought. As it turned out, not much that I took could have been safely left. Perhaps the rod cases or the setting pole were superfluous and maybe there were lighter vessels for our whiskey. It would have been nice to have a few additional red and white spoons for the trout. Still, humping that load makes you ponder what you agree to take on.

In embarking on this journey as intensely as I have, I sometimes wonder at the route that brought me to pursue the trail. Although I am generally fairly competent, I am also a pretty ambitious and curious person, eager to learn and try to solve tough problems with hard work—to really *do* things with my life. This desire to do things is my greatest strength and perhaps one of my greater weaknesses. It is a character flaw that opens new doors and invites disaster at most turns. In my drive to do what I seek to accomplish, I forget that others share my journey and that their stamina and goals may differ from mine.

The workaholism that seems to characterize my career runs the risk of harming my family and burning me out, but the fun of doing many different things excites me and keeps me going.

> Throughout our trip we commented on the superb natural beauty of the area. Just at the tree line the scenery was reminiscent of both the mountains of the West with sparse trees set amongst barren hilltops, and the coast of Maine with rocky islands facing an immense lake of frigid water. The Pretty River flowed cold and fast with the clearest water we had ever seen. The fishing was superb, the area desolate and magnificent. Our trip led us down 35 miles of the Pretty River, back up another channel of it and into another watershed, never visited by whites as far as we knew. While we faced no hardships for which we were unprepared, we changed plans several times. We chose not to push on beyond a falls because we had to be back for our plane and didn't want to risk the weather. ("Discretion is the better part of valor," as Falstaff said.) We chose not to travel down North River but to better explore North River Lake and were glad we did as we found some wonderful fishing.

Unless I am actually doing something, working hard, grasping for understanding of situations no matter what the effort, I feel I am standing still. There is too much to be done to improve our educational system to allow us the opportunity to stand still for very long. Trying to understand myself is a tough thing to do. It forces me to confront those aspects of myself that I haven't liked, those things I have done wrong. By persevering at it, though, I have experienced great exhilaration.

> Buck and I had a wonderful time there. He was thoroughly in his element and I've never seen him more relaxed and happy. He took pictures, climbed an impressively high hill, located a back pond and walked in to cast (unsuccessfully). (From Tulp's journal, August 11, 1992)

Return and Reflection

Tulp and I drove through the night on our return to Radisson
via Stéfan's Beaver, stopped and slept briefly, and drove the
remaining 20 hours as a straight shot. A long, straight shot.
Once home, I vegged for 2 days, not answering the phone,
watching old movies, and hoping my wife and kids would be
back from Florida early. Why do I need to veg after a long trip?
I should be rested and whole, but it takes longer for the effects
of the trip to sink in and they never quite leave.

Well into the fall I was drawing on the feelings of calm
and peace that I had found within myself at Pretty River. I
wasn't ready to head back, but knew I would be sooner or
later. Tulp and I corresponded, swapped photos, and I gave a
couple dozen slide shows to a variety of people before turning
my head to getting back up there. Over the winter I ordered
maps of the lower Pretty River, for the area beyond the falls
and down to Hudson's Bay. I rekindled my letter writing with
my footloose pen pals in Canada and convinced Tulp that another night spent drinking wine at Lu's house would be in
order this summer as we plan a somewhat more ambitious
trip for summer 1994.

Where has this part of the journey brought me? What goals have I
achieved that I otherwise would not? Am I better off as the result of
the effort? Will I continue to follow this path, choose another, or end
my journeying? Was it worth it? Who can say in the long run whether
or not efforts pay off in results that can be weighed and measured in
quantities like pounds of sugar and salt? Learning is measured up
and down and from left to right, inside and out, and yet the more we
measure the less we seem to know. The lessons of my efforts to be a
better principal seem to require a "vegging" period; they creep into
my consciousness at unexpected times and in unexpected forms, reminding me always of what I have to learn.

So What Is It I Have Learned?

I have learned that leaders must be the model for others' learning. My teachers, as difficult as they might be, must be given the opportunity to see themselves as learners. They must have the chance to talk about what they have learned and get from me the personal support necessary when the journey gets as tough as it can get.

I have learned that the process of writing can record thoughts to make them "reflect on-able" in the future. Discussing writing is as important as the writing itself, and the discussion is as important to teachers and leaders as it is to our students. Writing clarifies thoughts and opens them up to scrutiny in a way that dialogue never will. I've used reflective writing as a mirror in which I can clearly see myself. I must say that it has been easier for me to write about my troubles than my strengths. As a result of my recent experiences with both the Academy and the Writers' Collaborative, I find it easier to focus on the strengths that need to be utilized, rather than the weaknesses to be eradicated.

I have learned to treat teachers, parents, and others as well as I treat my students: to listen deliberately and act upon what they say to me. I haven't deliberately slighted adults. I simply find it easier to judge how kids function and harder to gauge the needs of adults. I have increased self-confidence in interpersonal work. I see myself now as being able to effect deliberate and lasting change in myself and others. I have become a more thoughtful and deliberate leader. I bring a greater degree of patience and understanding of other people's needs. I respond to my staff, parents, and students in ways that are meaningful to *them*, rather than me.

My personal life often reflects my need for the challenge of juggling many things. The trick has always been to strike a balance between all the things I love. I realize now that I can't hope to balance them all, but must blend them instead. The experiences shared with my colleagues and the greater degree of self-satisfaction have helped me come to grips with why I work these crazy hours. I accept that some of them are simply beyond my control.

I prize my time with my family, focus on them, and maintain them as the highest priority. I also recognize that part of me is ambitious and hard working. That's who I am. I've come to realize that seeing "the problem" as an opportunity to grow and taking the small breaks makes a difference in my level of satisfaction. I'm not trying anymore to maintain two separate lives, but one reasonably sane one. The problem for me has always been finding out what makes me happy *and* sane. It has been for me a remarkable experience to give up fighting between the two aspects of myself that always have been in conflict—the "me" at work and the "me" at home. I hope they have blended more closely together.

It seems to me that this constant tension between home and school will always be part of the problem for leaders of any type. To attempt to enact a vision, indeed to have a vision of what things should be like in my school, is to challenge myself to work hard to realize it. What I continue to lack is a personal vision of what my own life should be like. How to find that vision is one of my next steps.

> As we sat and waited for Stéfan at the end of our adventure, we took a look at the map and talked about what we missed by not heading down the Pretty River beyond the falls. We both agreed that it had been a mistake not to take the chance by paddling downstream a bit farther. Prudent, perhaps, but a mistake nonetheless. Tulp and I looked over the map and talked about seeing it the next time we were here. On every trip I've gone on in the real wilderness, there has been a stream that beckoned that we didn't follow, a carry into a pretty looking lake that we were too tired to make, a goal that we had set that we didn't achieve. Tulp and I have never talked about the other opportunities we missed, but I'm sure he has a list like mine. I'd never like to end a trip without one, for as long as there are those beckoning streams and uncarried paths, I'll have a reason to dream over my maps in January and picture in my mind what it would be like.

OUR JOURNEY:
Notes From the Writers'
Collaborative Log

A principal who served as cofacilitator of the Writers' Collaborative shares his journal about the Collaborative's activities and process.

George F. Marnik

The idea of writing about leadership challenges was embedded in the very nature of the Maine Academy for School Leaders itself. We had experienced firsthand the benefits of writing about our leadership in schools. The Writers' Collaborative provided us the opportunity to continue building on our relationships with one another and, as stated by Gordon Donaldson at our first meeting, "to participate in a monthly gathering for the purpose of reflecting on each others' writing and moving each person's writing forward to the point where it is a free-standing autobiographical description of an important learning episode in our development as leaders."

In the following pages, you'll glimpse into the life of the Collaborative as it evolved over the 9 months of its existence. As one of the organizers and facilitators of the Collaborative, I kept detailed notes of our meetings and shared these with other members through a narrative journal that provided a history of our time with one another. The following excerpts from this log, while hardly an exhaustive reporting of events, will provide insights into the growth of this reflective practice group. I have chosen these excerpts from each session's journal entry because they illustrate the flavor of the leadership issues facing members, the feeling tone of the group, the major struggles of writing about such challenges, and the growth and development of the group itself.

Friday, December 10, 1993

Despite a cold winter rain, 14 people gathered for the organizational meeting of the Writers' Collaborative. Gordon set the tone for our work together when he opened the session by talking about this opportunity as "a collaborative effort and not a class in writing. In that way it will be a continuation of the Academy experience and up to each of us to structure it to work."

The group began by establishing the following purposes:

1. Support the learning of Collaborative members.
2. Provide school leaders a supportive colleague-critic community as they strive to improve their leadership in specific ways.
3. Encourage exploration of written forms of reflection, expression, and "benchmarking" of the journey towards improved leadership.
4. Produce vivid stories of leadership growth told in the first-person voices of members that reflect the varieties of role, style, leadership challenges, personality, and school settings present in the collaborative's membership.
5. Integrate some parts of these stories into a publication.

We wrestled with how the Collaborative was going to work. The nature of feedback about one's writing that both supports and challenges each person was seen as a critical element to our success. How we functioned and the structure that supported our purposes were means to an end, but a means that needed to be firmly grounded in bonds of trust so that each person would be able to write about genuine challenges they faced and, ultimately, grow through the sharing of that writing.

Thursday, January 13, 1994

Snow and bitter cold now held Maine in their grip. Inside our room the feelings being shared were intense and warmed the heart. Our session started with a roundtable sharing of what was currently facing each of us in our lives. Then Julia led the group of a dozen people in an activity designed to further promote trust building by asking each of us to share what we had learned from a mistake we had made in our work lives. These recollections evolved into oral storytelling in which people shared an intimate moment in their lives as professionals. We could all relate to many of the stories and spent some time afterward examining their common themes. The personal voices and honesty inherent in these stories were precisely what we all wanted to capture in our writing. As one member summarized the experience: "The Collaborative is not a workshop on leadership practice. It is a means to facilitate our own reflection, to answer the question, How can I be supportive and assist you in finding your voice . . . your way?"

After a bowl of hot soup and a sandwich, we began the afternoon with Sally leading us in a discussion of what it means to be a "community of writers." We talked about writing and the anxieties some of us face during this process. We explored a variety of methods of gaining feedback on our writing based on our shifting needs and established the norm that it was incumbent on the writer to structure the kind of feedback he or she wanted at the time. The bottom line was that our final products were to be "a collection of voices about real experiences . . . stories that ring with clarity and authenticity." The group also talked about our audience and struggled with who we were writing for. The words of one person summed up the feelings of many when she said, "Through my writing I can better see who I am. This will be helpful to me . . . and to others."

Monday, February 7, 1994

February was upon us. Only seven members of the Collaborative were able to attend this day-long session. Because of the low turnout, we revisited our agenda and decided to spend the majority of the day reading each others' works-in-progress as a group. This would allow plenty of time for feedback, and such an approach would give everyone the advantage of hearing what people were focusing on in their writing. So we read, responded, conversed, and then repeated the cycle with another person. Common themes emerged in these initial drafts: working with difficult colleagues, self-doubts about one's own competencies as a leader, and the joys and frustrations of school change efforts.

Wednesday, March 9, 1994

The Collaborative next met in Augusta. Over coffee we spent the first half hour chatting with one another and getting caught up on each others' lives. We then set the structure for the rest of the day: the reading of each person's writing piece, with the authors establishing the kind of feedback they felt was necessary.

Our straightforward plan for the day quickly took a divergent road when the first person, Elizabeth, pushed the conversation in the direction of the process she was experiencing as she wrote about her leadership. Her issues about the effects of school change efforts were certainly perplexing and thus good fodder for thought. As she said, "The problem is so complicated. I can't begin to see through to the bottom of it. I'm muddling through but only at the very beginning of something." Voicing her concerns reflected what she had been writing about recently and echoed feelings many of us were experiencing in our own work. In fact, these ideas and drafts were so generic to working in schools that many of us thought about ourselves and our own schools as we read each others' writing pieces.

During the course of the day, other themes emerged in our writing and conversation:

- As we advocate for change in our schools, what is really lasting about our efforts?

- What is teacher leadership?
- How do we distinguish between the formal leadership position and personal style?
- How do I gauge my success as a leader?
- What controls the directions we pursue as school leaders?
- Does having a title in a school end up being more harmful than good?
- What is the nature of how relationships exist in schools? How can they evolve so that they are more constructive?
- As learners ourselves, how do we recover from our mistakes and outlive our past reputations? How do our past experiences impact our present-day reactions?
- How can we best break the norms and end the paralysis of our inaction? As the fabric of our school culture stretches, when will it break?

We ended the day by discussing a pestering issue: membership. Our attendance had fluctuated between 8 and 12 at each of our sessions. Why so few? It certainly required a high level of commitment to keep writing and exploring this medium as a valid way to improve our leadership practice. The day-to-day realities and demands of schools continued to determine the priorities for our time. While we struggled with this tug-of-war, questions of confidentiality, voice, purpose, and audience continued to form a strong undercurrent.

Saturday, April 9, 1994

The sun peeked through the clouds and the crocuses poked their first buds through the slowly warming ground. At long last a touch of spring was in the air as we gathered at Sally's century-old farmhouse for our monthly meeting.

We quickly became immersed in a discussion that focused on the benefits of reflective writing when stacked up against the day-to-day demands on our time. Some members expressed a sense of impatience with the time it takes to write and work back through a situation or challenge that had already occurred and been resolved, at least to a workable extent. Martha summarized some of the frustration when she likened the process to "driving over the same road again. . . . I might gain some new insights but I've already processed the event and drawn my conclusions. It's hard to continue to bother with it." Don expressed the counter argument: "I see it as thinking through my writing. It helps to clarify events for me. This stuff really works!" The debate continued with the advantages and challenges of writing about our practice tugging at us.

During our ensuing conversations and reading of each others' pieces we found that we were focusing on a common struggle: how to define, redefine, and act upon our relationships with others in our schools. We ended the day where we began. Feeling the need to push our writing forward, we talked about expectations for our next meeting and the possibility of a 2-day, overnight session in June. Our hope was that such immersion in our writing would allow us to block out much of the interference we had talked about earlier in the day.

Tuesday, May 10, 1994

We gathered in Augusta once again. It was a day that people watched both the sky and the earth: an early afternoon annular eclipse of the sun in Maine and the eclipse of apartheid in South Africa with the inauguration of Nelson Mandela.

Nine of us were present, and our opening time to check in with one another became a time to vent our frustrations with schools and share our thoughts in what had become a trusting and supportive environment. One member shares that she "feels a burning sensation from my throat to the pit of my stomach" as she struggles with how to shift the norms of her school toward more ethically defensible and respectful practices. Another member offers some solace: "This writing helps me to process my feelings, to get it out there to examine." Julia counters with an admission, common to some others in the group, that she was awake last night until after 11:00 p.m. working on her writing piece because of the need that she felt to "come with something and not let others down." She states the conundrum succinctly when she raises the question, "How do we integrate the value of writing into our busy lives and move beyond it being a task to be done by a certain date to it being an integral part of our learning?" The lack of norms in our schools that value such thought and work rears its ugly head again!

Over lunch, details about our 2-day retreat for June were discussed and finalized. It was agreed that everyone "would arrive with 'final' drafts of a piece of writing." These "stand-alone" pieces would be critiqued with time allowances for revision and further feedback over the 2 days. It was hoped that the intensity of working together in such a format would push people over the hump and help them to complete their "stories of leadership challenges."

Friday-Saturday, June 24-25, 1994

The Kennedy Conference Center in Nobelboro was a super location for our two day retreat! The facility and peaceful setting overlooking the lake edged by tall white pines helped us do the reflective work we had planned for ourselves.

We began by tackling the question, "What does a 'stand-alone' product look like?" Our discussion led to three conclusions:

1. *Format*: Each individual case needs to identify a story or theme and provide some sense of a beginning, middle, and end, even though the ongoing nature of these leadership challenges often mitigates against such linearity and conclusiveness.
2. *The reflective voice:* Our writing must capture the nuances of our own learning and growth and each author's personal style of writing—both in terms of the particular leadership challenge we are focusing on and the process of reflection and writing in our lives.
3. *Depth of writing:* We need to include adequate context and detail in each piece so that readers know what happened, but not so much that the story becomes confused and our learning is obscured.

We then turned to reading each others' pieces, jotting down notes for later discussion, and gathering to critique each person's work. While working on each piece as a group, we continued to see differences among individuals about their approach to such reflective writing:

Norma: Writing about such issues requires a courageous act . . .
    even in a supportive group like this. For me writing is a
    struggle. . . . It is hard to enjoy even though it does help
    me to clarify issues . . . in retrospect.
Don: I really enjoy writing. . . . It helps me to process the issues
    that are staring me in the face. . . . It is truly enjoyable.
Ann: It's hard to continue to revise when I own so much of
    what is there on paper. . . . Rethinking it is a challenge.

After a wonderful dinner, individuals returned to their writing
and worked on revisions based on the afternoon's feedback. We also
conferenced in pairs as people refined their efforts further. Finally,
the call of loons on the lake and stars poking through a cloudy sky
tempted us to the deck for further conversation before retiring.

On Saturday we awoke to a gray, damp mist and a large snapping
turtle laying eggs within sight of the front door. After a hearty breakfast, people returned to their individual rewrites and feedback from
others. By midmorning when we gathered as a group to report on our
progress, everyone talked about the "big leap forward" their pieces
had taken. Drafts were shared orally with one another, further suggestions made, and people talked about the newfound "aha's in my
understanding of what happened a few months ago that I only see
now through my writing and this conversation." The stress and bur-
dens associated with being a leader were a common theme in our
writing and conversation.

Thursday, July 14, 1994

We met in Round Pound at the Anchor Inn on a "finestkind" Maine
day—the sun was shining, the sky clear, sailboats bobbed at anchor in
the harbor, and work boats and their crews engaged in their liveli-
hood.

We outlined our feedback cycle for one another and quickly fell
into a conversation about issues related to format and publishing of
our book. Confidentiality and ethical considerations were of the greatest concern. We stressed the need for the introduction to directly address the "code of silence" that we seldom break in writing about
personal, and often painful, stories of leadership challenges in our

schools. It was our hope that Roland Barth, who would be joining us midafternoon, would write about this critical issue in the introductory piece he had agreed to pen and add to our efforts.

After a delicious lunch, Roland arrived by dinghy from his sailboat where he had spent the last few days cruising Muscongus Bay. He launched into his portion of the day with us by framing his view of reading our writing from the perspective of "individual pieces and their fit as a collective whole." His impressions of our work are most easily summarized as a series of points for our further consideration:

1. "I admire those that take the risk to write about practice since schools are such great places to hide."

2. Writing about schools can be seen as "war stories" (description only) versus "craft knowledge" (description and analysis). Many of our pieces end too abruptly and would benefit from more analysis, for example, "I learned . . ." or answers to the question, "So what?"

3. As writers we need to be aware of the shifting back and forth in our work between generalizations and specifics. They need to complement one another and not become too heavily weighted in one direction or the other.

4. We need to ask ourselves, "What is the title of my piece?" to help identify the theme of our story. We can also achieve greater focus in our writing if we reread it and ask ourselves, "Is my piece a mile wide and an inch deep, or is it an inch wide and a mile deep?"

5. *Economy* is critical in our use of language. "It is dangerous to fall in love with your own words. . . . Keep the tomatoes, but pick out the weeds."

6. The importance of the first paragraph cannot be overstressed. It must be "unlocking and inviting to the reader." It needs to answer two questions. "Do I want to read this?" and "Will I have to work too hard?"

7. "The burden on you is to bring life to the writing." To this end, creating actors and actresses in our writing who use language through direct quotes that are woven throughout the story is very important. Simply describing scenarios pales in comparison.

8. The audience we are writing for is often ambiguous. We should ask ourselves, "Who do we want to shake with this?" A clearly identified audience also helps in the editing process as we work to produce a crisp narrative. The audience we are writing for will probably vary among our pieces. In other words, "The fly that you're going to lay in that pool needs to be the one that is going to hook that trout."

9. Use metaphors! They say so much to the reader so quickly.

10. Be honest in our writing and accurately describe and share what we are *doing, learning,* and *feeling*. We need to "name the reality" for those who haven't or can't. Such honesty brings the author and the story to life.

Roland summarized his thoughts on our work as "an exciting new genre of writing for practitioners." He urged us to continue with our struggles leading in schools and to think of our work together over the past year as a

- Writing workshop
- Support group
- Seminar in meaning-making

A Retrospective View

Fall has returned to Maine and the final versions of writers' pieces have arrived on our desks. One last reading and revision as a part of the editing process and these stories of the challenges faced by a small group of school leaders will go into print.

Many nuances of reflective practice emerged for us during our time together as companions on this journey. Members of the Writers' Collaborative asked for and received much more than feedback on their writing. Writing was only the first step in a process—a journey inward to help us confront what we faced on the outside. Once a work-in-progress was read, the feedback on the writing often took a backseat to talking through the issues raised by the thoughts shared on paper. Emotional support, brainstorming ideas, and problem solving became an integral part of our time together. We coalesced as fellow travelers.

We were really writing about challenges of school leadership as a way to work through our concerns. These were real issues with real people. As writers we wanted reactions to our work as leaders in the situations we were describing. The group reaction then became the impetus for further reflection and eventual rewriting. Most important, our work together became a vehicle through which individuals could approach a struggle they faced with a fresh perspective. Working through a leadership issue with a group of colleagues away from the hectic life of school gradually showed us how our feelings, thoughts, and behaviors wer being influenced by people and decisions in our workplace. Time, further conversation, and more writing then helped us gain a measure of comfort and control over our own leadership and how we confronted what lay before us. We emerged feeling replenished and more confident that we really were making a difference in the lives of our colleagues and—most of all—school children.

WRITING FOR
PROFESSIONAL GROWTH:
A Double-Edged Sword

*A cofacilitator of the Collaborative reflects on the power and pitfalls of
leaders writing from their personal experience for a public audience.*

Gordon A. Donaldson, Jr.

The major goal of our Writers' Collaborative was to advance our learning through writing. We all had written about our leadership in self-
reflective journals and portfolios while members of the Leadership
Academy. This writing, while not painless, nourished our learning
and our leadership enough so we wanted to join this Collaborative.

But the Collaborative had a second goal: to share the products of
our writing with professional—and perhaps other public—audiences.
Whereas our Academy writing had been for ourselves, we Collaborative members hoped we could eventually make our learning available publicly to others in printed form. This greatly changed the
experience and process of our writing. We all found that writing about
our leadership for the public was a double-edged sword: On one hand,
the more personal our investigations into our actions, feelings, and

beliefs as leaders became, the more we learned and the more useful it was to our practice. On the other hand, the more personal (and inter-personal) our reflections became, the riskier it became to make these investigations public.

This invisible but very real double-edged sword made writing and publishing these reflections somewhat hazardous. When added to the other demands of writing about practice—finding the time, energy, self-discipline, and disposition to think anew about oneself—these hazards are more than enough to keep many school leaders from even trying to write. As our articles demonstrate, we found it extraordinarily valuable to work past these hazards. We include this brief article to help future leader-writers to do likewise in the hope that they will eventually share their own learning experiences with professional audiences.

Learning About Yourself
as a Leader Can Be Very Personal

Our sessions weren't like lots of professional meetings we've attended where people are swapping trade secrets, telling war stories, or learning from experts. Each time we met, we designated "floor time" for each member to talk about (and talk through) issues he or she confronted in being a better leader. Each of us was invited to find an aspect of our leadership that was significant *to us* and to use the group and the writing to understand it better.

As you have seen in the articles here, this environment led us on quite personal journeys. Although we often talked about new educational and leadership practices, the nub of our leadership investigations lay within us: How am *I* going to make these practices succeed? How am *I* going to bring these teachers and parents around? How can *I* build collaboration among these diverse teachers? We all saw leadership not merely as what needed to be fixed in others or in programs at school. It was also about us, our responsibility for the status quo, and our competence at leading others to make things better for kids. This was hard work; it often brought us face-to-face with our failures, our doubts, and our blind spots in dealing with others.

Pursuing Leadership Questions
Makes You Feel Vulnerable

What made this work even harder was that the issues we often tackled were among the messiest or most troublesome we faced at work. We seemed to say to one another, "If I'm going to put time into attending the Collaborative and writing for it, I damn well want to focus on something that'll make a difference." More often than not, the "make-a-difference" issues were rooted in questions about our own effectiveness as leaders: Has my work leading this committee really helped it progress? Is it my failure that this member of my department is making kids and parents angry? Why do I always feel so inadequate after a faculty meeting where teachers attacked one another? Did I support this shaky staff member in ways that will help his or her performance?

Such questions made us feel vulnerable. They were hatched from our self-doubts as leaders. Pain, failure, and embarrassment lurked in the answers to them. It took a certain amount of resilience simply to want to write about these matters. It took even more to want to share that writing with the rest of the group.

To a person, though, the greatest rewards of the Collaborative came from grappling with these personal/professional issues in the safe setting of our group. We could think out loud and in writing without worrying about offending anyone. More important, we could express the feelings that accompanied our leadership experiences. This often meant we shared with each other anger over an unresponsive staff member, fear of a manipulative boss, frustration at not meeting our own high expectations, and joy at a hard-won accomplishment. We came to know and trust each other enough so that the personal vulnerability we might ordinarily feel in sharing these aspects of leadership largely evaporated.

A Second, More Troubling Kind of Vulnerability

Though difficult, writing about these gnawing personal leadership questions was tremendously therapeutic for most of us. The monthly writing-discussion-writing cycle gave us all a wonderful chance to grapple not only with our own issues but with each others'.

As our comfort with one another and our confidence in the confidentiality of our group grew, we were increasingly able to share without "editing" how we felt, what we thought, and what we did as leaders and to be blunt about our doubts and questions.

While this helped to evaporate our sense of personal vulnerability, it did not have the same effect on a second kind of vulnerability. Many of the situations we wrote and talked about revolved around the behavior of other people in our schools. In exploring leadership experiences that were problematic for us, we nearly always focused on other people who impeded our ability to lead effectively: a group of parents or teachers, or a specific parent or teacher, a school board member, a custodian, or a superintendent.

None of us felt totally comfortable with this: It always felt like we might be violating confidentialities just by mentioning someone whose identity was known or could be deduced. We all felt vulnerable *for having talked about others as "the problem"*; was it right to expose what others did or said? And we worried that our own agendas and emotions might be unfairly distorting the picture of this person or this group; were we scapegoating in order to conceal our own failures? Many of us felt disloyal to our schools, colleagues, and towns, as if this honest talk was made dishonest by its "behind-your-back" quality.

Is This Stuff Fit for Public Consumption?

Making colleagues or stakeholders vulnerable by talking about their foibles and their unresponsiveness to our leadership efforts was a choice we each made as we decided what to write and talk about. Similarly, within the Collaborative, we could make our own choices about how self-revealing to be. But when we thought about making our writing public, the picture changed radically. Did we have a right to publicly represent a colleague as a blocker, a manipulator, a reactionary, a dolt? Did we want to expose ourselves and our innermost thoughts and concerns about our leadership to an audience of unknowns or, worse, to the audiences in our schools?

Clearly, some fundamental ethical and legal principles come into play here. Another person's professional reputation might be at risk if he or she is exposed in our writing as, for instance, a laggard, a non-team-player, an incompetent teacher, an improper influence on kids. (Wait a minute, you say, in this latter case, don't we have an obligation to expose?) We also might be transgressing personal liberties by revealing information that we learned through a privileged professional relationship. If we publish, we not only might be liable as authors but our districts might be as well (especially if we are administrators). And another thing: Might publication of personally revealing information about colleagues have serious reverberations at work when people there read it?

We run risks to ourselves as well. If we publish accounts of our thoughts, worries, feelings, self-doubts, beliefs, and actions as leaders, we swing a camera in on many things about us that others don't often see, hear, or feel. What conclusions about *us* might others reach from this messy "inside" footage? That we're insecure? Vindictive? Narrow-minded? Power-hungry? Unworthy of trust? Lost?

Playing With a Double-Edged Sword

These observations bring our dilemma into stark relief. As "learning leaders," we know the value of public learning and believe in the importance of sharing our lessons with others. But the lessons are often very personal, and they carry these vulnerabilities to ourselves and to those we work with. This is probably why so little writing about leadership learning ever sees the light of day.

The stories you have read in this book have all had to pass the double-edged-sword test to the satisfaction of their authors. This means that some perspectives, some events, and some personalities have probably been glossed over in order to protect everyone. It also means that authors have, in the final drafts, been unable to express everything they have learned about themselves and their leadership. We have edited them to "protect the innocent" and, inevitably, we have shielded some of the "guilty" as well.

And it means that you have not read all our stories. One Collaborative member wrote about a leadership issue of such personal significance and that involved other personalities to such a degree that she chose not to publish it. Others opted to edit out vital sections because to make them public would expose other people, their words and actions, and the effects they had not only on the author but on others at school. In several cases, the learning process was so personally engrossing and, on some level, so painful that it was not possible to relate it in a form that others could understand or the author could feel satisfied with.

The net result of all this is that we shall continue to have partial stories and in some cases no stories from leaders who have important lessons to share with us. The double-edged sword will continue to trim, cleave, and skewer valuable parts of our knowledge about leadership, keeping them from professional (and public) circulation. We are left with a literature about school leadership that is tidier, more interpersonally and personally sterile, and less truly indicative of the experience of leading than we would like.

Our leaders, we think, have displayed an unusual level of courage and stamina in sharing what they have in this volume. It is worth remembering, too, that the greatest learning value of our Collaborative experience stemmed from the writing-discussing-writing cycle made possible by the closeness, honesty, and trust of our group. Many of us believe that if leaders are to continue growing in their work, they need such safe colleague-critic circles throughout their careers.

Norma Richard, the author of our first story, is very fond of this line of Eudora Welty's: "The events in our lives happen in a sequence of time, but in their significance to ourselves, they find their own order . . . and the continuous thread of revelation" (in Sumrall, 1992, p. 79). In the final analysis, busy school leaders like Norma need most a professional circle in which the events of their leadership lives can "find their own order" so that the "thread of revelation" can continue for them.

We hope that you have gained from the threads we have revealed in our stories. And we trust that by spinning those threads for others outside our circle, we have encouraged you to examine the events in your own leadership lives so you, too, might find and share your own threads of revelation more publicly.

Reference

Sumrall, A. C. (Ed.) (1992). *Write to the heart: Wit and wisdom of women writers*. Freedom, CA: Crossing.

A GLOSSARY OF MASL TERMS

Terminology from our common experience in the Maine Academy for School Leaders appears in these articles. The following definitions and descriptions will prove helpful.

Roland Barth, David Sanderson, Lucianne Carmichael: Consultants to MASL.

Bowdoin Institute: A week-long residential Academy activity at Bowdoin College in July 1992.

I-C-I—Interpersonal-Cognitive-Intrapersonal: The MASL program was based on a model that holds that leadership and leadership development occur simultaneously in these three dimensions of functioning. Leaders' knowledge and activity—and thus their learning—must be understood in all three dimensions.

LDP—Leadership Development Plan: A written growth plan specifying each Academy member's goals for improving their leadership behaviors and implementing those plans in each of the I-C-I domains.

MASL—Maine Academy for School Leaders: A leadership development program organized through the Maine Leadership Consortium, November 1991 - June 1993.

MNSL—Maine Network of School Leaders: The network formed by alumni of the Academy and others, June 1993.

Portfolio: A leadership portfolio developed by each member to assess and demonstrate the development of his or her leadership skills and knowledge over the course of the Academy.

S & D Teams—Support and Development Teams: Groups of three or four Academy members that met, observed one another, and served as colleague-critics for one another's efforts to grow as leaders.